GOD
HERE
AND
NOW

GOD HERE AND NOW

The Christian view of God
by Peter Toon

M.A., B.D., M.Th.,
D. Phil.

Tyndale House
Publishers, Inc.
Wheaton, Illinois

Library of Congress
Catalog Card Number 78-66201
ISBN 0-8423-1046-0, paper
Copyright © 1979
by Peter Toon
All rights reserved

First printing,
August 1979
Printed in the
United States of America

CONTENTS

ACKNOWLEDGMENTS

I have to thank the students of Oak Hill College for helping me choose the method I have adopted in presenting the doctrine of God. They conducted some market research for me among young people whom they met in pastoral work. The Principal, Canon David Wheaton, not only suggested the title but also made comments on the contents of the book. Also, Richard Ginn, B.D., has been a great help in assisting me to work out my ideas and put them on paper.

I dedicate this book to Walter Persram of Toronto, Canada. In the midst of personal suffering he has come to know the *God* who is certainly *here* with us *now*.

The biblical quotations are from the Revised Standard Version.

Peter Toon
Oak Hill Theological College
London, England

INTRODUCTION

A Christian is a person whom God has brought into a particular relationship with himself. God calls and brings people to himself to be his disciples in many different ways. A few people become Christians suddenly. A few reach Christian commitment at the end of their lives. But for most Christians it is usually the case that their arrival at true discipleship follows a gradual process of change spread over a significant period of time.

A Christian, having been brought by God into a relationship with himself, enjoys an ongoing relationship with God. The description of this relationship by the individual Christian varies from person to person. For example, some call it "peace in the heart," others "joy on the lips"; some call it "purpose in life," others "freedom from bondage." Yet others give an account of their experience which includes all of these.

A Christian needs to be able to relate his present experience of God to the words and acts of God recorded in the Bible. It is both tempting and easy to regard God's activity in Jewish history in the distant past as in some way remote from the Christian's present experience of God. So one purpose of this book is to show that God's speech and acts as recorded in the Bible provide the framework within which the Christian is to understand his own ongoing relationship with God.

The Christian Church labored for many years to produce creeds and statements of faith which expressed the best possible understanding of the God of whom we read in the Bible. When properly understood, the Apostles', Nicene, and Athanasian Creeds, all produced before A.D. 500, remain a satisfactory and coherent interpretation of major themes of the books of the Bible. As these Creeds show, the Church has understood God to have revealed himself and to be a Trinity-in-Unity and a Unity-in-Trinity. The doctrine of the Holy Trinity—Father, Son, and Holy Spirit —is not a riddle to baffle would-be seekers after truth. Rather, the Holy Trinity is the Christian name and understanding of the God who has called the believer into a relationship with himself, to be a disciple of Jesus Christ, and to be filled with the Spirit.

The experience of God enjoyed by the apostles and their congregations was the experience of God in Trinity. Their work of evangelism and teaching was in the context of baptizing disciples in "the name of the Father and of the Son and of the Holy Spirit" (Matt. 28:19). The prayer of each for the other was: "The grace of the Lord Jesus Christ and the love of God and the fellowship of the Holy Spirit be with you all" (2 Cor. 13:14). The salvation received and enjoyed by the Christians came from the God who is Three in One and One in Three. The Christians were "chosen and destined by God the Father and sanctified by the Spirit for obedience to Jesus Christ and for sprinkling with his blood" (1 Pet. 1:2). And the source of the different gifts functioning within the individual churches was the triune God. Paul wrote, "there are varieties of gifts, but the same Spirit; and there are varieties of service, but the same Lord; and there are varieties of working, but it is the same God who inspires them all in every one" (1 Cor. 12:4-6).

The Jews did not know that God is One in Three, for God did not reveal this truth to mankind during the period which the Old Testament describes. The basic belief of Israelites and Jews is contained in what they call the *shema:* "Hear, O Israel: The Lord our God is one Lord; and you shall love the Lord your God with all your heart, and with all your soul, and with all your might" (Deut. 6:4, 5). Yet the God whom Israelites knew, and who is now known by Christians, is one and the same Lord. We are able to enjoy a richer knowledge of God because the Son of God became man, and as Jesus, the Christ, showed us what God is like.

So the God whom Moses, David, and Elijah knew is the same God who was known by Paul and John; and he is the same God whom Christians today know. Because of this fact, the way God has made himself known to Israelites and Jews is always of help to us. And also, the way God made himself known through Jesus and in the teaching of the apostles is always of help to us. God guided his people to write the books of the Bible so that Christians always would have a sure record of what he is like and how he is to be known, loved, and served.

The method of presentation which we shall follow in this book is based upon three factors. First of all, we will begin each chapter with the experience of the Christian in his relationship to God. Then we will turn to the record of God's acts and words, written in the Bible, in order to deepen our knowledge of God. Finally, we will seek to discover how our knowledge of God, gained from the Bible, deepens our experience and understanding of God. In other words, our concern is with our commitment to the reality of God and the implications of his reality for today. In facing these implications, we have to face current questions relating to the problem of suffering, the possibility of miracles, and the nature of the gods of other religions.

ONE
God Is Alive

The committed Christian is aware of the presence of God in and around him; he is also conscious of the guidance of God in his life. The Christians who form the local church are conscious of God as they worship and serve him together. They know him as One who is very near to them and yet who is also beyond their reach, because he is so great and glorious.

There is never any discussion in the Scriptures concerning whether or not God exists. From the first words—"In the beginning God created the heavens and the earth" to the last—"the grace of the Lord Jesus be with all the saints. Amen."—the existence of God is taken for granted. We find that in the pages of the Bible it is assumed and proclaimed that the Lord God is totally alive; he is nothing less than the living God who enters into relationships with angels and human beings.

THE LIVING GOD OF THE OLD TESTAMENT

The strong convictions of the ancient Israelites
that their God was the living Lord comes
through the pages of the Old Testament in a
variety of ways. A very important passage is
Exodus 3:13-15:

> Then Moses said to God, "If I come to the
> people of Israel and say to them, 'The God of
> your fathers has sent me to you,' and they ask
> me, 'What is his name?' what shall I say to
> them?" God said to Moses, "I AM WHO I
> AM." And he said, "Say this to the people of
> Israel, 'I AM has sent me to you.' " God also
> said to Moses, "Say this to the people of
> Israel, 'The Lord, the God of your fathers, the
> God of Abraham, the God of Isaac, and the
> God of Jacob, has sent me to you': this is my
> name forever, and thus I am to be remembered
> throughout all generations."

The ancient peoples among whom the Israelites
lived believed that to know the name of their
God was to have direct access to him in order to
gain his help in battles, in the growth of vital
crops, and in the increase of their flocks and
herds. In this passage we find that Moses and the
tribes of Israel want to know their God's name,
and be like their neighbors who have names for
their gods. Therefore, he reveals it to them.
But in doing so, he gives Moses a far greater
disclosure than he could have expected. Let us
examine it.

First, God describes himself as the God of their

forefathers; the God who led, directed, and appeared to Abraham at Mamre (Gen. 15:1, ff.), to Isaac at Beersheba (Gen. 26:23, ff.), and to Jacob at Bethel (Gen. 28:13).

Second, he reveals his name. Just how it was pronounced in Hebrew we do not know, for all that we have in the Hebrew Bible are the consonants YHWH. Between these letters the vowels "a" and "e" are inserted so that it can be pronounced Yahweh. An older way of rendering the Hebrew consonants YHWH was the word Jehovah, which one finds in many theological books. Thus Yahweh and Jehovah are of identical meaning. When translating YHWH, different English versions adopt different words: the RSV translates it "Lord" (and on a few occasions "God"), (following the King James version), while the NEB uses "Jehovah" on five occasions and "Lord" or "God" the rest of the time. (It is an interesting exercise to read the introductions to the Old Testament in both the RSV and the NEB, as they give explanations of their translations of YHWH.) The best translation of YHWH appears to be "I am who I am," and the meaning is that God is the self-existent One. Nothing or no one made him; he needs no one; he is perfect in himself; he is entirely adequate in himself for the present and future. He is timeless and he is a Spirit: "God is Spirit," said Jesus, "and those who worship him must worship in spirit and truth" (John 4:24).

Yahweh is the name by which the one true God desired to be known. It is interesting to observe that in the Old Testament there are several *words* for God (e.g., *el* and *elohim*), but only one *name* for God, "Yahweh." The importance of this fact for us today is increased when we learn that the personal name in ancient times was seen as a description of the person's character and personality. A simple example is found in the book of Ruth. When the people of Bethlehem asked, "Is this Naomi?" she replied, "Do not call me *Naomi* [or, pleasant], call me *Mara* [bitter], for the Almighty has dealt very bitterly with me. I went away full, and the Lord has brought me back empty" (Ruth 1:20, 21). Therefore, Yahweh, "I AM WHO I AM," perfectly describes God's nature and character.

God's revealed name is of great importance. So the fourth commandment states: "You shall not take the name of the Lord your God in vain" (Exod. 20:7). So also the psalmist could write the following lines:

Teach me thy way, O Lord,
that I may walk in thy truth;
unite my heart to fear thy name.
I give thanks to thee, O Lord my God, with
my whole heart,
and I will glorify thy name for ever
(Psa. 86:11, 12).

The very name, Yahweh, declares that God is the living Lord.

Third, he is the God of action. He makes himself known in the affairs of men. In particular, he entered into a special relationship with the descendants of Abraham (Gen. 12:1, ff.) and will enter into a special agreement (covenant) with Moses and the people of Israel as they wait upon him at the foot of Mount Sinai (Exod. 19, 20). In Exodus 3:14, 15, God is telling Moses that he is the self-existent One, the living Lord, and they will know who he is by the actions he takes in history. Because of the covenant he makes with them, they will know that he is in complete control of the world. If they recognize his rule and obey his word, then they will always experience his help and guidance. If they choose to disobey him, then they will experience his judgment in terms of such things as plagues, famines, and defeat in battles.

Therefore, the true confession of faith of the people of Israel is that which they made in the presence of Elijah after the fire of the Lord had consumed the sacrifice: "The Lord, he is God; the Lord, he is God" (1 Kgs. 18:39). Also, in the words of the prophet Isaiah, the relation of the Lord to the people was as follows:

"You are my witnesses," says the Lord,
"and my servant whom I have chosen,
that you may know and believe me
and understand that I am He.
Before me no god was formed,
nor shall there be any after me.
I, I am the Lord,
and besides me there is no savior.
I declared and saved and proclaimed,
when there was no strange god among you
and you are my witnesses," says the Lord.

"I am God, and also henceforth I am He;
there is none who can deliver from my
   hand;
I work and who can hinder it?"
   (Isa. 43:10-13).

In short, Yahweh, the Lord, is alive and is in
control of the universe and its people.

Two expressions, fairly common in the Old
Testament, remind the reader that the God who
was dealing with Israel is the unique
self-existent One. They are: "as the Lord lives"
and "as I live, says the Lord God." The first
of these is common in the books of Samuel
(1 Sam. 14:39, 45; 19:6; 20:21; 25:26; 26:10, 16;
28:10; 29:6; 2 Sam. 4:9; 12:5; 14:11). An
examination of each of the contexts of this
expression will reveal two basic principles
underlying or associated with it. Usually the
expression presupposes that the living God has
entered into an agreement with the people of
Israel, that he is their God and they are his
people. So there is a backward look to the making
of this covenant at Sinai and to the obligations
involved in it (Exod. 20, ff.). Then there is
confidence in the present and future, for the God
who made the covenant remains constant. He
cannot change in himself; he is the Lord who will
always deal justly with his people.

If we read the story in 1 Samuel 14 of how
Jonathan disobeyed his father Saul, then on the
occasions (vv. 39 and 45) when Saul uses the
expression "as the Lord lives" we can see that he

is appealing to the covenant relationship in which the people stand before God, for he sees in this covenant both human obligations and the divine initiative.

The other expression "as I live, says the Lord God" has a similar meaning and is found particularly in the prophecies of Ezekiel (14:16, 18, 20; 16:48; 17:16, 19; 18:3; 20:3, 33; 33:11, 27; 34:8; 35:6, 11). Both the covenant relationship and the certainty of God's help are illustrated by Ezekiel 20:32-34. The background to this passage is that the Jews are in exile in Babylon and are contemplating the possibility of adopting the ways and worship of those among whom they live. God is speaking and he says:

> What is in your mind shall never happen—the thought, "Let us be like the nations, like the tribes of the countries, and worship wood and stone." As I live, says the Lord God, surely with a mighty hand and an outstretched arm, and with wrath poured out, I will be king over you. I will bring you out from the peoples and gather you out of the countries where you are scattered, and with a mighty hand and an outstretched arm, and with wrath poured out . . .

The habit of the writers of the Old Testament, both in this passage and elsewhere, of talking about God as though he had human parts, will be discussed later in this chapter.

The reality of the living God was also the basis

for some of the fine prayers of the book of
Psalms. For example,

> As a hart longs for flowing streams,
> so longs my soul for thee, O God.
> My soul thirsts for God, for the living God.
> When shall I come and behold the face of God?
>   (42:1, 2).

and,

> How lovely is thy dwelling place, O Lord
>   of hosts!
> My soul longs, yea, faints for the courts of
>   the Lord;
> my heart and flesh sing for joy to the living
>   God (84:1, 2).

The true Israelite who believed in the existence
of the living Lord saw it as his duty and his joy
to worship and seek after him.

THE LIVING GOD OF THE NEW TESTAMENT

The living God whom the Israelites worshiped
is the God of Christians. Continuing the
emphasis of the Old Testament, the expression
"the living God" is found nearly twenty times
in the New Testament. It occurs, for example,
when a contrast is being made between the cold,
lifeless idols of wood, metal, or stone, from
whose worship converts turned in order to honor
the true God as made known in Jesus Christ.
At Lystra, Paul and Barnabas were taken as

personifications of the gods Zeus and Hermes. This shocked them, so they told the crowd that they were merely men whose only special claim to fame was that they brought good news "that you should turn from these vain things [idols] to a living God who made the heaven and the earth and the sea and all that is in them" (Acts 14:15). In describing the conversion of the Christians in the church at Thessalonica, Paul wrote that they had turned "to God from idols, to serve a living and true God" (1 Thess. 1:9).

The whole of the New Testament may be simply explained as a description of the living God in the character and actions of Jesus Christ and in the ministry of the Holy Spirit within the Church and world. To put this another way it may be claimed that the self-existent One, Yahweh, is seen in the New Testament as the self-existent Trinity, for he makes himself known in his saving activity as Father, Son, and Holy Spirit.

In their encounter with Jesus Christ, in their relationship through him with the Father, and in their experience of the power and presence of the Holy Spirit, the early Christians recognized that God himself—the God of Abraham, Moses, and Elijah—was bringing men and women into fellowship with himself. To them he was the living, triune God. They remembered the words of Jesus that he and the Father are one in their divine nature (John 10:30) and that the Spirit who gives eternal life to the believer and cohesion to the fellowship of Christians comes from the Father and the Son (John 14:26). The Christians knew and worshiped God as One who was manifested as Three. They did not attempt to explain how God could be distinctly Three and still be One. The Trinity is a great mystery; yet, it is an unavoidable reality.

During the three or four centuries following the apostolic period, the Church had to give much thought to the stating of the doctrine of the Trinity. This task was necessary because various types of false teaching were being propagated in the churches. The expositions which the bishops have left for us in the Nicene and Athanasian Creeds are not meant to provide perfect descriptions of God. Rather they are to be seen as very useful guidelines for us to use as we read the Scriptures and seek to understand what they teach. (See the Appendix.)

One of the themes of the Epistle to the Hebrews is that if the God of Christians is truly the living and only Lord, then a merely formal type of Christianity will not do. To serve the living God is to live in obedience to God, with joy and perseverance. Having been cleansed by the blood of Christ, Christians are urged: "purify your conscience from dead works to serve the living God" (9:14), that is, serve him with living works of obedience and mercy. To pretend to be a Christian and to live as though the commands of Christ and the availability of grace did not exist was perilous, for "It is a fearful thing to fall into the hands of the living God" (10:31).

In summary, when it is said that God is alive, it is said that he is fully alive to and in himself in his Unity in Trinity, and that he is alive to believers who enjoy a relationship with him.

GOD IS PERSONAL

When someone today has an intense sense of belonging to God he will probably describe his experience in terms which could give the impression that God is a superior human being. Such expressions as "I talk with the Lord," "I walk with the Lord," and "I met the Lord," as well as the ones in which God is the subject— for example, "The Lord guides me"—only make sense to the speakers and hearers if they are aware that language is being used in a peculiar way and is the language of Christian commitment. God is not a being with whom I actually walk down the street or to whom I actually talk on the telephone or greet in my office. The one God is personal Spirit. Jesus taught us to pray "Our Father," and such language is necessarily personal. (We shall return to study the Fatherhood of God in chapter seven.)

As we read the Old Testament we find that the Israelites also found it easiest to describe God in personal terms. They had a definite, covenantal relationship with Yahweh, and when they came to refer to him as their living Lord they spoke and wrote as if he were a magnificent human being. So we find that God speaks (Gen. 2:16, 18), hears (Gen. 16:11; Exod. 2:24), sees (Gen. 11:5; Psa. 14:2; 53:2), smells (Gen. 8:21; Lev. 26:31), laughs (Psa. 37:13; 59:8), and even whistles (Isa.

5:26). He has a heart (Gen. 6:6; 1 Sam. 13:14),
face (Exod. 33:14, ff,; Job 1:11), eyes (Psa. 34:15;
66:7), ears (Num. 11:18; Psa. 34:15), nostrils
(Exod. 15:8; Psa. 18:15), hands (Psa. 119:73), arms
(Isa. 52:10), feet (Psa. 18:9). He walks (Lev. 26:12,
24) and goes to war (Exod. 15:3; 17:16).

There are many moving descriptions of God in
the Old Testament which are written in this
style. Experts call this use of human features and
characteristics to describe God "anthropomorphism" (*anthropos* = a man; *morphe* = shape;
thus, describing God in the shape of a man).
Possibly no part of the Old Testament uses more
anthropomorphisms than Psalm 18.

In my distress I called upon the Lord;
to my God I cried for help.
From his temple he heard my voice,
and my cry to him reached his ears.
Then the earth reeled and rocked;
the foundations also of the mountains
    trembled
and quaked, because he was angry.
Smoke went up from his nostrils,
and devouring fire from his mouth;
glowing coals flamed forth from him.
He bowed the heavens, and came down;
thick darkness was under his feet.
He rode on a cherub, and flew;
he came swiftly upon the wings of the wind
    (Psa. 18:6-10).

In this short extract we note that God hears
with ears, he is angry and sends smoke through

his nostrils, and fire from his mouth, he descends making use of his feet, he rides, flies, and moves swiftly.

Sometimes people claim that the anthropomorphisms belong to the early parts of the Old Testament when ideas were primitive, and that they gradually disappeared in the later more sophisticated writings. They point to the expression "the Lord God walking in the garden" of Eden (Gen. 3:8) as an example of naive thinking and then claim that in Isaiah there are majestic descriptions of God without anthropomorphisms. But this is hardly true. Here are extracts from Isaiah 40 and 42.

Behold, the Lord God comes with might,
and his arm rules for him;
behold, his reward is with him,
and his recompense before him.
He will feed his flock like a shepherd,
he will gather the lambs in his arms,
He will carry them in his bosom,
and gently lead those that are with young
    (Isa. 40:10, 11).

The Lord goes forth like a mighty man,
like a man of war he stirs up his fury;
he cries out, he shouts aloud,
he shows himself mighty against his foes
    (Isa. 42:13).

In these three verses God pays a visit, has arms and uses them, cries and shouts, and is victorious in battles.

It is written of Yahweh that he knew Moses
face to face (Deut. 34:10), that he spoke with him
mouth to mouth (Num. 12:8), and that he spoke
to Moses like a man to his friend (Exod. 33:11).
The best way to explain this language is to state
that the references to parts of the human body
and bodily functions are not actual, literal
descriptions of God, but rather figurative
expressions which describe his qualities, making
use of poetic license. The meaning of the images
is in most cases perfectly clear. Let us illustrate
this point.

One apparently crude description of God is the
reference to his nostrils. "At the blast of thy
nostrils the waters piled up" (Exod. 15:8).
Breathing heavily and snorting with the nostrils
were for the ancient Hebrews bodily expressions
of anger—similar to the raising of eyebrows or a
facial frown to the average Westerner. The
Hebrew word for nostril, *aph*, also means
"wrath," so when Moses or an Israelite thought
of God's anger, he thought of God snorting
through his nostrils.

For ancient people the human arm symbolized
strength and power because everything had to
be lifted manually before the advent of
technology. So Jeremiah wrote:

Cursed is the man who trusts in man
and makes flesh his arm,
whose heart turns away from the Lord
    (Jer. 17:5).

And Isaiah wrote:

> The Lord has bared his holy arm
> before the eyes of all the nations;
> and all the ends of the earth shall see
> the salvation of our God (Isa. 52:10).

Surely what Isaiah means here is that Yahweh provided helping power to his covenant people.

The human hand also symbolized human might and power. To be in the hands of Yahweh, and in particular in his right hand, means to experience his divine power.

> Thy right hand, O Lord, glorious in power,
> thy right hand, O Lord, shatters the enemy
>   (Exod. 15:6).
> The sea is his, for he made it;
> for his hands formed the dry land (Psa. 95:5).

Similar points could be made with respect to the eyes of the Lord (Psa. 116:15) and the ears of the Lord (Psa. 18:6).

We all know that Yahweh, the self-existent Spirit and Holy Trinity, is not a magnificent human being; no committed Israelite or Christian ever taught that! But Yahweh is personal in the sense that we can have a relationship with him and he with us. The only words which we have in our everyday language are those meant to describe people and objects, emotions and attitudes, ideas and principles.

Our words are basically earthbound; they are designed to describe normal, everyday things. So when we come to speak or write about God who is not subject to time and space but who is, nevertheless, personal Spirit, we find it easiest to describe him in language that we ordinarily use in our relationships with people.

When we reflect on our descriptions of God we recognize that we are using ordinary language in a special way, but we rarely try to define exactly how we are using the language. Personalizing God seems as natural to us as it did to the ancient Israelites and the early Christians. They experienced God in such a real way that it made sense to them to describe him in words which normally referred to living human beings.

Despite the fact that biblical authors wrote anthropomorphically, the representation of God in any human or animal form was never condoned. One of the Ten Commandments (Exod. 20:4) and much of the teaching of the prophets (e.g., Isa. 46:5, ff.) were aimed at prohibiting the representation of Yahweh in the form of any finite, created being. However, the great "I AM WHO I AM" had to be described in human words simply because of the limits of our language.

We must recognize that religious symbols are not necessarily idolatrous. The ark of the covenant in and after the time of Moses was a symbol of the presence of Yahweh and of his covenant relationship with the people. The bread and wine of Holy Communion are symbols of the Lord Jesus Christ who died for our sins.

Symbols help in directing our minds toward the reality of God and his love for us.

People descend into idolatry when they try to localize and control God instead of being controlled and guided by him. Idolatry characterizes decadent religion (Rom. 1:18, ff.), and can only be avoided through a trustful relationship with the living God. When the Israelites turned to the gods of their neighbors they were condemned by God, although they managed to worship Yahweh alongside these other deities (see the stories in Judges). Likewise, Christians come under the chastisement of God when they, too, attempt to live with a divided loyalty—"You cannot serve God and mammon," said Jesus (Matt. 6:24).

The living God is the God of true Christian experience. To say that God is personal is to say that Christians can now have fellowship with him. If God were impersonal, then it would be impossible to have a dynamic experience of him. The Christian experience of God does not guarantee the existence of God; this is because experience is subjective and can be misinterpreted. Experience can, however, confirm for the Christian what he believes on other grounds.

When Christians discuss the salient features of the Christian life they resort to their own familiar jargon to enable them to talk about their own life lived in a relationship with God. Christians make use of the language of emotions ("on fire with love for God"), of politics ("he sets me free"), of taverns ("drunk with the Spirit"), and so on.

It is often difficult for non-Christians to cut through this tangle of language to know what is central to the Christian life. The sober-minded agnostic may be suspicious of emotions, distrustful of politics, and contemptuous of pubs and taverns; thus, it is necessary to be clear as to what is at the core of our Christian experience. The core of this experience is that *God is alive.* Because God is alive, the Christian is alive; and the individual Christian expresses what this life is in his own way, though he often makes use of language passed down for centuries in the Church.

THE GOD OF OTHER RELIGIONS?

A question frequently asked today concerns the identity of the God worshiped by Christians, Muslims, Hindus, and other religious people. Do they all worship the same God? In short, if Christians are alive to the living God, is God alive to the non-Christians? Let us look briefly, for example, at the doctrine of God found in Hinduism and Islam. In the next chapter we shall consider their holy books.

In Hinduism, according to the teaching of the Vedas (the earliest Hindu scriptures), God is the true absolute which they call Brahman. Brahman is not a personal spirit but an abstract, unknown reality. It is the subtle essence of the whole world. The whole cosmos proceeds from Brahman like a spider's web flows out of the spider itself. Brahman is everywhere but no one can see, touch, smell, taste, or know its presence.

It is in any object or in any living being. It is beyond the threefold relationship of seer, sight, and seen; knower, knowledge, and the known. It is essentially unknowable. All our approaches to it are imperfect and all our attempts to describe it are in vain. No moral qualities can be ascribed to Brahman. It is neither holy nor unholy, neither loving nor unloving.

Alongside this concept of the Absolute, the practice of worshiping a variety of gods and goddesses exists among Hindus. If all the village deities of India are taken into account, this number traditionally comes to 330,000,000, which seems unbelievable to a Westerner. While belief in one absolute and many gods seems like two contradictory concepts, it does not pose a problem to most Hindus. It is apparently easy for them to think of few or many gods as being absorbed into one universal reality, Brahman. Thus, the multitude of gods and goddesses are nothing but manifestations of the one Absolute.

This very brief summary reveals that there is little or no correspondence between the Hindus' concept of God and the Christian faith. There is no equivalent of Brahman in Christian thought; neither is there the belief in a great variety of gods and goddesses. In dialogue with Hindus and those attracted by Hindu mysticism, we must humbly seek to demonstrate that we worship a living God whom we know and with whom we enter into personal fellowship.

Islam is totally committed to the unity and transcendence of God. God is one and has no partner, no wife and no children; he is totally different from his creatures. A new convert is enrolled on the confession of the creed that "There is no God but one God and Muhammad is the prophet of God." God is not only different in kind from his creatures, but he is also above all of them. The attitudes and actions of his creatures cannot affect him, for he is wholly independent of them. His will is supreme and cannot be changed. The proper relation to him is that of submission (Islam means submission). Any forgiveness and punishment meted out to creatures is according to this supreme will. And everything is pre-ordained. "Allah wills what he wills." Thus the God of Islam is the God of judgment and justice; on the day of judgment, Allah will judge all men according to their works.

It can be said that the God of Islam is the God of the Old Testament, but without the attribute which the old translations called "loving-kindness." This is true despite the fact that Muslims call God "the Compassionate." Totally absent from Islam is the God of grace, the God who lovingly enters into the world of time and space to save and help those he has created. So, while the Muslim worships the God whom Jews and Christians worship, he worships in partial ignorance. Although he knows of the justice and wrath of God, he knows little about the mercy of God—especially the mercy displayed in Jesus Christ.

God is alive and enters into living relationships with sinful human beings. This is the glorious message of the Christian Bible and of the Christian Church. In relationship with the Father, Son, and Holy Spirit, the sinner has eternal life. And, this Lord, to whom the sinner is related, is the Lord who speaks to him.

In the next chapter, we shall study the God who speaks.

TWO
God Is Speaking

Before a sermon a preacher usually prays that the Lord will speak through his exposition of Scripture to the minds and hearts of his hearers. Sometimes hearers of a sermon report their conviction that God has actually spoken to them, making clearer his will for their lives or for the church. When a spiritual gift is exercised within the Christian congregation (1 Cor. 12:4, ff.), it is believed by those present that God is speaking to one or more members of the fellowship.

At the personal level the Christian often believes that in his daily time of devotion—whether it includes reading a Scripture, meditation, or prayer—the Lord speaks to him. Also, as Paul taught in Romans 8:14, ff., he often has a vital inward conviction that God is actually saying to him, "You are my child and I love you."

In chapter one we looked at the use of anthropomorphic language about God. To say that "God is speaking" or "God has spoken" is clearly to use an anthropomorphism. When we say "God is speaking" we imply that God still communicates with men. To say that God has spoken once and for all time is not to contradict this fact; rather, it is to draw attention to the distinction between the way God speaks to a Christian, or to the Christian fellowship today, and the way he spoke to those whose experience is recorded in the books we call Holy Scripture.

Certainly it is the same living God who spoke to Moses and Hosea who now speaks to the Christian. Of this there is no doubt; but the speech of God recorded in the Bible is special. It is special, and in some senses unique, because it belongs to and explains a series of mighty acts of God which are unique and which were the means God himself chose to bring salvation into the world. These events—for example, the call of Abraham, the Exodus of Israel from Egypt, the making of the Covenant with Israel at Sinai, the Incarnation of the Son of God and his resurrection, together with the founding of the Church by the apostles—cannot be repeated; and neither can the word of the Lord which accompanied them. What God said and did through Israel, in Jesus Christ, and by the apostles, he did once, for all, and for ever, in order to make it possible for human beings of all times and places to enjoy fellowship with himself. His revelation in word and event is, by its very nature, unrepeatable.

God's words to the individual Christian now, though precious to the one who receives them, do not belong to the same order and uniqueness. They belong to what may be termed the appropriation and reception of salvation, that same salvation which is recorded and described in the words of Scripture.

Perhaps to some readers what has been written so far in this chapter appears "old-fashioned." They have probably heard clergymen or ministers say from the pulpit that God does not reveal himself in words and in speech. God did not speak to men in the past and he does not do so in the present. These preachers probably believe that God only reveals himself in mighty acts (e.g., the deliverance of Israel from Egypt), or in personal disclosures (e.g., to Paul on the road to Damascus). They tell their hearers that God did not really speak, and does not truly speak, directly to men and women. When questioned, such ministers usually explain that the recorded words of God to Moses (e.g., Exod. 19:3, ff.), or to David (2 Sam. 2:1), or to Jeremiah (Jer. 1:4, ff.), or to Jesus (Matt. 3:17), are merely records of what the writers thought that God could be (or should be) saying to these people. The implication of this approach may be that God has never spoken in a manner which human minds can understand and appreciate. The books of the Bible are then seen as human witnesses, human accounts, and human responses to God's mighty acts or personal disclosures. In this view the Bible is a very valuable volume, but in it there is no record of God's speech to man; it only contains man's speech about God and man's idea of what God would say if ever he were to speak to man.

This way of thinking about God's relation to humanity has the effect of making churches weak and unsure of what they are meant to do and proclaim in the world. And, as we shall see, it is unacceptable! Let us take a simple example to show how an event without an authoritative interpretation is an event which is open to a variety of interpretations, and is, therefore, meaningless.

If I live in Edinburgh and get in my car and drive to London, neighbors might ask my wife why I had not gone by train or plane. The reason for my going in my car is certainly known to me and hopefully also to my wife, but others have to make guesses. One could say that I had relatives in Yorkshire and was probably intending to visit them; another could say that I was a collector of books and probably intended to buy a small library and bring it back with me; yet another could say that I was anticipating the possibility of a strike on the railways and so wanted to be sure of return travel. My own reason might be quite different; it might simply be that I wanted to give my car a good test because I loved to drive. If I did not tell people this, they could not be sure that this was my reason for going by car.

The same principle applies to the great events

of the Bible. Take the Exodus. The departure from Egypt can be explained in several ways; for example, as one of the many migrations of tribes in ancient times. Unless God spoke to Moses and told him what he was doing and why he was doing it, those who were a part of the Exodus, those who heard or read about it afterward, and those who read about it now could never be sure of having the right interpretation of it. Take also the resurrection of Jesus of Nazareth. The disappearance of his body and the claims of certain people to have seen him raised from death are open to several interpretations. But God gave us, through Jesus himself and also through his apostles, words to explain and understand what the resurrection was all about (e.g., Luke 24; 1 Cor. 15; Rom. 6:1-11). Therefore, it has been the claim of the Church, ever since the Day of Pentecost (Acts 2), that God has not left us uninformed as to what his mighty acts of salvation mean. He has given us in sentences which we can understand an account of the meaning of his saving activity.

The New Testament claims that God clearly spoke to and through Moses, the prophets, and other leaders in Israel. And, if we believe in the living Lord, then this way chosen by God to communicate with human beings makes good sense. Peter wrote that "men moved by the Holy Spirit spoke from God" (2 Pet. 1:21), and the writer of the Epistle to the Hebrews confidently affirmed that "In many and various ways God spoke of old to our fathers by the prophets" (Heb. 1:1). Take the example of Jeremiah. He was very conscious of his youthful inexperience and protested to God that he could not possibly be his messenger. But the Lord told him that he was not to think of his age "for to all to whom I send you you shall go and whatever I command you you shall speak" (Jer. 1:7).

Not once, but many times, we read in the Old Testament that "the word of the Lord came to" a certain prophet. Often when the prophets spoke they introduced what they had to say with the important words, "Thus says the Lord." The experience of Amos, the small-time farmer, as a receiver and bearer of the words of the Lord, was unforgettable and vivid:

> The lion has roared; who will not fear?
> The Lord God has spoken; who can but
>   prophesy? (Amos 3:8).

Other prophets had similar experiences of the powerful word of God; for example, Isaiah's vision (chap. 6) and Ezekiel's vision (chap. 2, ff.).

Because God spoke to them and through them, Moses and the prophets gave what must be called authoritative explanations of the saving activity of God within history. By listening to them in their own times, or by reading their oracles, the Israelites of old and we today can understand the meaning of the covenant relation between Yahweh and his people.

At this point we can pause for a moment to consider just how important the spoken word was in Israelite society. When words were spoken with intent and purpose they were held to be effective words. For example, when Isaac found he had blessed the wrong son (Gen. 27:33-37), he was unable to recall his words. His only course was to give another blessing to Esau (Gen. 27:39, 40). Perhaps it is easiest for us to think of the "effective word" by recalling how in a modern comic-strip in a newspaper the characters' words are contained in a circle above their heads. In this way their words appear to have solidity and permanence. Spoken words exist outside the person who spoke them and they cannot be pushed back into the speaker's mouth. With this background we can, perhaps, better understand the words of God through Isaiah when he said: "So shall my word be that goes forth from my mouth; it shall not return to me empty, but it shall accomplish that which I purpose, and prosper in the thing for which I sent it" (Isa. 55:11).

As Christians, we claim that God spoke his final word in and through Jesus Christ. The New Testament is full of words of God spoken by Christ, and the words of God spoken and written by apostles of Christ as they were inspired by the Holy Spirit. The Son of God became a man and was called Jesus of Nazareth. So when he spoke, though he used human words in a specific language, nevertheless his message was from God. While Jesus did not introduce everything he had to say by claiming it was the word of God, he did sometimes make it clear that the words he spoke were straight from God.

On one occasion, in the Temple of Jerusalem, he spoke these words to the Jews, who were astonished that he had such wisdom: "My teaching is not mine, but his who sent me; if any man's will is to do his will, he shall know whether the teaching is from God or whether I am speaking on my own authority" (John 7:16). Here he claimed that his words were from the heavenly Father, the Father whom these Jews, as well as Jesus himself, should serve. On another occasion he stated: "He who sent me is true, and I declare to the world what I have heard from him" (John 8:26). To reject the word of Jesus was a serious matter, for it involved rejecting the words of God. To demonstrate this, Jesus told the story of the two men who built houses, one on sand and one on rock (Matt. 7:21-27; Luke 6:46-49). Only the one whose house had a firm foundation survived.

Apart from the actual words which Jesus spoke, there is a vital sense in which he himself, in all he was and did, was a total portrayal of God's dynamic word. One biblical writer clearly expressed this truth by saying: "in these last days he has spoken to us by a Son" (Heb. 1:2), while another wrote that "the Word became flesh" (John 1:14). God's clearest and fullest revelation of himself is in his incarnate Son. Unlike others, the actions of Jesus did not speak louder than his words. Rather his actions perfectly complemented his words.

Throughout his ministry Jesus taught, preached, and acted out, the word of God. Yet all this was inadequate to express the full word of God in him as the incarnate Son. His self-expression reached its perfection in his death and resurrection. What words could not say was said at Calvary. All that was incommunicable in the divine communication expressed itself in the arms outstretched, the body drained of blood, and the heart pierced by the spear. The word of love was given over fully to men. The revelation in word was consummated and sealed by revelation in suffering, death, and resurrection.

The words of the apostles of Christ were also words from God, for they were in the power of, and under the guidance of, the Holy Spirit. After Jesus' ascension, the Holy Spirit was sent from the Father as a guide for the apostles and the churches they founded (John 14:26; 15:26; 16:12-15; Acts 2). Paul spoke of the mystery of Christ, the meaning of his saving work for men, being revealed to the apostles and early prophets by the Holy Spirit (Eph. 3:5).

Let us now summarize the argument of this section. God is the Lord who actually speaks to chosen men and women in words they can understand. He spoke in days of old specifically to explain his saving intentions and activity within history, to make known the type of personal and community life and worship he wanted from his chosen people, and to declare his plans and purpose for the future. In Jesus Christ and through the apostles God spoke his final words; final, that is, in the sense that they are the last of an accumulation of words from him. By means of them, the earlier words recorded in the Old Testament make full sense. Since all the words recorded in both Old and New Testaments are joined to unique, saving events—particularly the incarnation of Christ—they cannot be repeated. They are final, authoritative and true. They remain in force as long as the world continues to exist.

God's character is totally reliable and trustworthy; thus his words of promise, of challenge, and of moral demand always remain true. God, the Lord, also speaks today to the individual Christian and to the local church, applying the unique words of the once-for-all revelation to individual circumstances and needs.

Having claimed that God's word is reliable and trustworthy, we need to make a few comments on the use of the Old Testament. Jesus Christ said that he came not to destroy the Old Testament but to fulfill (fill with clearer meaning) the contents of the Law and Prophets (Matt. 5:17). So when we read the Bible we remember that much of what the Old Testament teaches is given a fuller interpretation in the New Testament. Also, as the letter to the Hebrews makes perfectly clear, the whole sacrificial system of worship associated with the Temple pointed toward, and was fulfilled in, Jesus Christ. Further, since much of the Law of Moses had to do with what we would now call civil and ceremonial laws, this part of the word of God does not have an immediate applicability for us today. It had relevance when all the people of God were in one nation. Now the people of God are found in many nations of various races. Thus, while we believe that all Scripture is the word of God, we read the Old Testament in the light of the New.

God's word through the biblical writers is God's word for today just as much as it was God's word for yesterday. Because God is not absent from the world, but is present as Holy Spirit, the word spoken long ago is still the word of the Lord for today.

It is, therefore, quite proper to think of the contents of the Bible as the preaching and teaching of God to the Church, the world, and the individual, in all generations. God the Father preaches God the Son, in the power of God the Holy Spirit. This last short, but important sentence, needs a few words of explanation. The Old Testament looks forward to the New Testament; and the heart of the New Testament is Jesus Christ. So it can be said that the whole Bible is about Jesus Christ, the incarnate Son of God. God the Father sent the Son into the world (John 3:16) and, by the work of the Holy Spirit—both before and after the incarnation—made sure that men were able to understand what he said about his Son and were able to write it down accurately.

But the work of the Spirit is not finished when he has helped men to make a faithful record of God's words. He is present in the churches and in the hearts of individuals in order to give understanding to the reader and hearer of the words of God, and also to make the words powerfully relevant for today. Thus God the Holy Trinity, Yahweh, the Lord, speaks today. God the Father preaches Jesus Christ, the Son, by the power of the Spirit to all faithful hearers and readers of the Scriptures. Sometimes God's preaching to us falls upon deaf ears; but at other times our ears and hearts are open and we are able to hear and receive the words of God.

It is of great importance in evangelism to know that one of the activities of the Holy Spirit is to convince hearers of the word of God that they are sinners, that they stand in need of the free gift of the righteousness of Christ, and that, through Christ, God speaks of judgment for sin (John 16:8-10). The Spirit takes the words of God spoken by the evangelist and applies them to the hearts of hearers. So it is that "the word of God is living and active, sharper than any two-edged sword" (Heb. 4:12).

Having made this very important point that the contents of Holy Scripture are the message which God is speaking and preaching to us today, we have to add a few comments concerning the best way to hear his speech to us. We must always bear in mind that the speech of God recorded in the Bible was originally transmitted to men and women who spoke in Hebrew, Aramaic, or Greek. It was also delivered in different centuries and in different circumstances—e.g., to Abraham in ancient Haran, to Moses in the desert of Sinai, to Ezekiel, in Babylonia, and to Paul in Greece or Italy. Happily, people who read English have a good supply of translations and some excellent paraphrases.

This provision of good translations and paraphrases is extremely valuable, but, in itself, it is not enough to enable us to hear the word of God from Scripture today. We have to bring to our reading of Scripture a desire to get to know its general contents and themes so that we understand the general principles of how God works in history. This means that we do not treat the Bible as merely a collection of unrelated texts which jump up to meet our needs at any given time or in a specific crisis. Rather, we read a whole section at a time whenever possible so that we have a general understanding of the context in which the words of God were originally spoken. This may mean reading the whole of the life of Abraham or the whole Epistle of Paul to Galatia. As we prayerfully do this God speaks to us.

In an old, much-used sermon entitled "A fruitful exhortation to the reading and knowledge of Holy Scripture" (printed in the *Church of England Book of Homilies* of 1562) there is some sound advice. It begins:

> Unto a Christian man there can be nothing either more necessary or profitable than the knowledge of Holy Scripture, forasmuch as in it is contained God's true word, setting forth his glory and also man's duty. And there is no truth nor doctrine necessary for our justification and everlasting salvation, but that is, or may be, drawn out of that fountain and well of truth. Therefore, as many as be desirous to enter into the right and perfect way unto God, must apply their minds to know Holy Scripture; without the which, they can

neither sufficiently know God and his will, neither their office and duty. And as drink is pleasant to them that be dry, and meat to them that be hungry; so is the reading, hearing, searching and studying of Holy Scripture, to them that be desirous to know God, or themselves, and to do his will.

And a little later we read the following:

These books, therefore, ought to be much in our hands, in our eyes, in our ears, in our mouths, but most of all in our hearts. For the Scripture of God is the heavenly meat of our souls: the hearing and keeping of it maketh us blessed, sanctifieth us, and maketh us holy; it turneth our souls; it is a light lantern to our feet. It is a sure, steadfast, and everlasting instrument of salvation; it giveth wisdom to the humble and lowly hearts; it comforteth, maketh glad, cheereth, and cherisheth our conscience; it is a more excellent jewel or treasure than any gold or precious stone; it is more sweet than honey or honey-comb; it is called the best part, which Mary did choose, for it hath in it everlasting comfort.

The sermon proceeds to deal with two "vain excuses" put forward by ordinary people against the regular reading of Holy Scripture. One excuse is that they are afraid that by reading of Scripture they will fall into error through misunderstanding it. The other excuse is that

Scripture is very difficult and only should be read by ministers and learned men.

In order to avoid falling into error by misunderstanding Scripture the writer of the homily states:

> Read it humbly with a meek and a lowly heart, to the intent you may glorify God and not yourself with the knowledge of it; and read it not without daily praying to God that he would direct your reading to good effect; and take it upon you to expound it no further than you can plainly understand it. For, as St. Augustine saith, "the knowledge of Holy Scripture is a great, large and a high place; but the door is very low, so that the high and arrogant man cannot run in; but he must stoop low, and humble himself, that shall enter into it." Presumption and arrogancy is the mother of all error; and humility needeth to fear no error.

With regard to the second excuse concerning the difficulty of Scripture we read:

> He that is so weak that he is not able to brook strong meat, yet he may suck the sweet and tender milk, and defer the rest until he wax stronger and come to more knowledge. For God receiveth the learned and unlearned and casteth away none, but is indifferent to all. And the Scripture is full, as well of low valleys, plain ways, and easy for every man to

use and walk in; as also of high hills and mountains, which few men can climb unto.

If a man finds parts of the Bible very difficult and prays for God's help, concludes the homily, God will either send him the help of a godly teacher (as he sent Philip to the Eunuch in the Acts of the Apostles) or illuminate his mind to understand.

But what about the word of the Lord which comes through the gifts of tongues or the word of prophecy? Is this extra revelation? From what has already been presented it follows that where God truly speaks in the operation of these gifts he speaks always in agreement with his word recorded in the Scriptures. The Holy Spirit speaking today never disagrees with that which he inspired men to write centuries ago. So the word of God through the exercise of the gifts of the Spirit in the Church will be either a declaration of what is already known in the Bible (by the experienced reader), or will be the application of principles laid down in Scripture to a specific situation known to one or all of those assembled. If anything is claimed to be from God which is obviously contrary to the teaching of God in Scripture, then we can be sure that the speech is not from God.

In waiting to hear the Lord's word and in listening to him, we must never forget that we are not perfect human beings, but sinners whom God is slowly making holy. Accordingly, our hearts and imaginations often deceive us and make us think that our own thoughts and desires are God's word to us. So we must always take great care and check as much as possible—by consulting older Christians, for example—before we make large claims concerning what God has said to us.

God is speaking. God has spoken. A Christian's present sense of hearing God speaking in sermons, through spiritual gifts, or in private prayer does not usurp the revelation of God in the Scriptures. Rather, his present initiative to man preserves and interprets his final written revelation from generation to generation. The revelation recorded in Scripture is authoritative for Christians; it is the rule of their faith, morality, and religious experience. The present experience of God enjoyed by Christians is God's commentary on the once-given revelation. To regard God's commentary on his revelation as simply a continuation of his revelation is a grievous error, for it allows us to suppose that our present experience of God is equally, or even more, significant than his original, unique revelation.

DOES GOD SPEAK THROUGH THE HOLY BOOKS OF OTHER RELIGIONS?

We have just expounded a very high view and estimate of the Christian Bible. Many Christians, aware that there are other holy books in the world which are deeply reverenced by thousands of people, ask the question: Is there a revelation of God recorded in the holy books of other religions and does God speak through these books?

In the last chapter we saw that there were different views and concepts of God in Hinduism, Islam, and Christianity. The basic reason for this difference is that the various holy books or scriptures expound and promote differing doctrines of God.

The Hindu scriptures were written mostly in the ancient language of Sanskrit over a period of more than two thousand years. They can be divided into two sections. The first is called "Sruti" which means "what is heard." The Vedas, which are four in number, belong to this section. They are considered the primary and final authority of religious truth. Hindus believe that the religious truths of the Vedas were given directly to the ancient seers, known as rishis, whose disciples recorded them. The second section is called "Smriti" which means "what is remembered." This section contains all the sacred books other than the Vedas, such as the law books known as the Manu; the epics—the Ramayana and the Mahabarata; and the Puranas which contain myths, stories, and legends. "Smriti" has only a secondary authority as it derives its authority from "Sruti."

Though Hindus believe that the Vedas are the final authority for religious, spiritual, and moral truths, it must be said that a purpose of the Vedas is not to be the means of revealing God to man. The Vedas are not the record of God's self-revelation but a collection of abstract and practical "truths." One of these truths is that while men should search for God they can never fully find him and they certainly cannot know him. The "avatars" or appearances of God in the world do not have the purpose of revealing God to men but rather of establishing justice and truth in a particular situation. So they are not to be compared to the incarnation of the Son of God.

Muslims believe that the Koran, which is their only holy book, is the final message of God to mankind and that Muhammad was the final messenger of God. It is also believed that the Koran was a revelation to Muhammad, being delivered to him by the angel, Gabriel. Before that time it existed, so Muslims claim, eternally in heaven and in the Arabic language. Except in the first chapter, which is a prayer addressed to God, God is the speaker. Just how greatly the Koran is reverenced by followers of Islam is seen in their discipline of reciting a section or verses from it five times daily in their prayers, and also in their efforts to memorize as many verses as possible. It is also seen in the fact that they observe strict silence when it is read aloud in public.

Muslims believe that there were a series of prophets, among whom was Jesus, but they claim that Muhammad is the last of them. However, they neither worship him nor any other teacher or prophet. They offer worship only to God, Allah.

The Koran has no "good news" of a God of grace who enters into this sinful world in order to be born as a man and share in our human condition, thus bringing us salvation. The God of Islam is the remote, stern, and just God, and his revelation through the prophets is based on this character.

Now we must try briefly to answer the question posed at the beginning of this section. In the Christian Bible, the self-revelation of God reaches its climax and focal point in the incarnation. Jesus Christ in his saving work of reconciling men to God revealed the character and purposes of God. In neither the Hindu holy books nor the Koran is there any revelation of this kind. Certainly in the Koran there are portions which parallel the Christian Old Testament, but there is nothing to compare with the fullness of the revelation of God in the New Testament.

THREE
God Is Active in Creation

Many Christians enjoy what we call in our churches "the harvest festival." They look forward to singing such a hymn as:

> We plough the fields and scatter
> The good seed on the land
> But it is fed and watered
> By God's almighty hand;
> He sends the snow in winter,
> The warmth to swell the grain.
> The breezes and the sunshine
> And soft refreshing rain.
>
> All good gifts around us
> Are sent from heaven above
> Then thank the Lord, O thank the Lord
> For all his love.

In such words as these we express the belief that the God whom we serve is the Creator and

Sustainer of our universe. Then, also, our present concern with conservation proceeds in Christian thinking from the belief that the God who created and now upholds the universe requires us to use the creation for ends which are pleasing to him, and are in accord with the nature of the created order.

CREATION AS PORTRAYED IN THE OLD TESTAMENT

The teaching of the Bible is that God is both Creator and Sustainer (Jer. 23:23; Psa. 29:8, 9; Isa. 40:26, 28-31). If for one second God ceased to support and control the vast universe in which we live, it would collapse and disintegrate. The changing of the seasons, the growth of seeds into plants, the birth of the lamb or the calf, the movement of the earth and stars, the ebb and flow of the tides, all are wholly and totally dependent upon the will of God. The fact that God was in charge of his universe was made clear to Noah after the flood; God told him that: "While the earth remains, seedtime and harvest, cold and heat, summer and winter, day and night, shall not cease" (Gen. 8:22). Much later, Jeremiah reported Yahweh as saying:

Thus says the Lord,
who gives the sun for light by day
and the fixed order of the moon
and the stars for light by night,
who stirs up the sea so that its waves roar—
the Lord of hosts is his name (Jer. 31:35).

For the Israelites, the creation of the world was the first mighty act of the Lord (Gen. 1).

Often the Israelites reminded themselves of God the Upholder of the universe by praising him as the Creator.

> O Lord God of hosts,
> who is mighty as thou art, O Lord;
> with thy faithfulness round about thee?
> Thou dost rule the raging of the sea,
> when its waves rise, thou stillest them
>   (Psa. 89:8, 9).

> The heavens are thine, the earth also is thine;
> the world and all that is in it,
> thou hast founded them.
> The north and the south, thou hast created
>   them;
> Tabor and Hermon joyously praise thy name
>   (Psa. 89:11, 12).

Then again:

> For the Lord is a great God,
> and a great King above all gods.
> In his hand are the depths of the earth;
> the heights of the mountains are his also.
> The sea is his, for he made it;
> for his hands formed the dry land.
> O come, let us worship and bow down,
> let us kneel before the Lord, our Maker!
> For he is our God,
> and we are the people of his pasture,
> and the sheep of his hand (Psa. 95:3-7).

We could give many more quotations from the Psalms where the joyful praise of God, Creator and Preserver, is often linked with praise of God the Redeemer (see next chapter).

For the writers of the Old Testament there was no doubt that God had made all things. In our modern terminology every atom and molecule, every electron and neutron, every part of the cosmos was made by God out of nothing. The technical Latin term for this action is *creatio ex nihilo* (creation out of nothing). The reader who looks at Genesis 1 and then reads the testimonies to creation which often occur in the books of the Old Testament is left with no doubt of the Israelites' conviction that God is the sole Creator of all that is. Addressing the Jews, God said through Isaiah: "Thus says the Lord, your Redeemer, who formed you from the womb: 'I am the Lord, who made all things, who stretched out the heavens alone, who spread out the earth—Who was with me?' " (Isa. 44:24).

When human beings make things, and this includes everything from a garden fence to a jumbo jet, they make them out of material that already exists—wood and nails in the case of the fence, and metals, plastics, and many other substances in the case of the jet. In fact, we have no experience of making something out of nothing. God's act of creation is unique, for he actually created out of nothing the energy and matter which constitutes the world as we know it.

This means that the world is totally dependent upon God for its existence and without him could not exist. When parents produce a child that child, after being dependent upon them, gradually becomes independent of them. But since God always gives and sustains human life we are always dependent upon him.

CREATION AS PORTRAYED IN THE NEW TESTAMENT

From the New Testament we learn that God the Son shared with God the Father in creation and also shares with God the Father in upholding the universe. Paul declared that for Christians there is "one God, the Father, from whom are all things and for whom we exist, and one Lord, Jesus Christ, through whom are all things and through whom we exist" (1 Cor. 8:6). John declared that "In the beginning was the Word, and the Word was with God, and the Word was God. He was in the beginning with God; all things were made through him, and without him was not anything made that was made. In him was life, and the life was the light of men" (John 1:1-4). The Word is the Son of God who "became flesh and dwelt among us."

In his Epistle to the Colossians, Paul joined together the work of the Son as Creator and Preserver of the universe: "He is the image of the invisible God, the first-born of all creation; for in him all things were created, in heaven and on earth, visible and invisible ... all things were created through him and for him. He is before all things, and in him all things hold together" (Col. 1:15-17). The writer of Hebrews wrote of the Son as the One "through whom also he [the Father] created the world" and who upholds "the universe by his word of power" (Heb. 1:1-3). Both the Old and New Testaments tell us that creation was achieved and is sustained by the powerful word of the Lord. "By the word of the Lord the heavens were made, and all their host by the breath of his mouth" (Psa. 33:6). The breath of the Lord is his Spirit (cf. Gen. 1:2). There are no explicit statements in the New Testament which proclaim the place of the Holy Spirit in the work of creation and the activity of upholding the universe. But there is much teaching that the Spirit is the one who is forming the new creation, which will replace this old one in which we live (Gal. 5:5). So we can rightly deduce that the One who is involved in the making of the new is also involved in the maintenance of the old, especially when the Old Testament states that he is (Gen. 1:2; Job 33:2, 3). We turn to the work of the Spirit in the new creation in the next chapter.

GOD AND HIS UNIVERSE

As Creator and Upholder, Yahweh is both with us and around us here on earth and far above and beyond us in heaven. He is able to be in the world, through the world, and also above the world because he is the Lord, self-existent Spirit. The psalmist wrote:

Whither shall I go from thy Spirit?
Or whither shall I flee from thy presence?
If I ascend to heaven, thou art there!

> If I make my bed in Sheol, thou art there!
> If I take the wings of the morning
> and dwell in the uttermost parts of the sea,
> even there thy hand shall lead me,
> and thy right hand shall hold me
> > (Psa. 139:7-10).

In a moving oracle Amos spoke for God,
declaring there was no place where one could
hide from Yahweh.

> Though they dig into Sheol,
> from there shall my hand take them;
> though they climb up to heaven,
> from there I will bring them down.
> Though they hide themselves on the top of
> > Carmel,
> from there I will search out and take them;
> and though they hide from my sight
> at the bottom of the sea,
> there I will command the serpent,
> and it shall bite them.
> And though they go into captivity
> before their enemies,
> there I will command the sword,
> and it shall slay them;
> and I will set my eyes upon them
> for evil and not for good (Amos 9:2-4).

The presence of God was everywhere in his
world.

Sometimes God made his presence very
obvious to the Israelites. In the burning bush
which was not consumed by fire (Exod. 3:3), in

the pillar of cloud and of fire which guided
the Israelite tribes by day and by night (Exod.
13:21; Num. 14:14), and in the luminous cloud
which descended upon the newly built Temple
of Solomon (1 Kgs. 8:10-12)—as it had done upon
the ancient tabernacle (Deut. 31:15)—the
presence of God was certainly known. It was
also specially mediated, symbolized, and known
by such physical manifestations as earthquakes,
fire, smoke, and thunder (e.g., Exod. 19:16-18;
20:18). Prophets experienced the power of the
Spirit and word of the Lord (2 Kgs. 3:11-20)
while the ancient charismatic leaders or judges
performed mighty exploits in the power of the
Lord (see the book of Judges).

Israelites were also very conscious that the
God who had entered into a covenant with
them was far removed from them. He was not
separated by a gulf that could be measured in
terms of thousands of miles but was separated
by the fact that he is Spirit and not governed by
or subject to time and space. So he can be called
"the high and lofty One who inhabits eternity,
whose name is Holy" (Isa. 57:15). For the
psalmist, God was exempt from all temporal
bonds. He is before, after, and independent of
every occurrence in time.

Lord, thou hast been our dwelling place
in all generations.
Before the mountains were brought forth,
or ever thou hadst formed the earth and the
world,
from everlasting to everlasting thou art God.

Thou turnest man back to the dust,
and sayest, "Turn back, O children of men!"
For a thousand years in thy sight
are but as yesterday when it is past,
or as a watch in the night (Psa. 90:1-4).

At the same time God is active in everything
that occurs. Amos asked,

Is a trumpet blown in a city,
and the people are not afraid?
Does evil befall a city,
unless the Lord has done it? (Amos 3:6).

The answer he expected was a certain "No";
God certainly is active all the time. Though he
is above the universe, he dwells with the lowly
and the humble. "For thus says the high and
lofty One who inhabits eternity, whose name is
Holy: 'I dwell in the high and holy place, and
also with him who is of a contrite and humble
spirit' " (Isa. 57:15).

Paul summarized the New Testament
portrayal of the relation of God to the created
universe when he wrote that there is "one
God and Father of us all, who is above all and
through all and in all" (Eph. 4:6). God is above
the universe in the sense of being external to it;
we pray, "Our Father who art in heaven,
Hallowed be thy name" (Matt. 6:9). God the
Son incarnate in Jesus Christ is the primary
means by which God is "through all." He is the
highest, the greatest, and the ultimate
expression of God. In the Garden of Gethsemane

63

he prayed "yet not what I will, but what Thou wilt" (Mark 14:36), and in all he did he perfectly fulfilled the will of God in word and action (cf. Heb. 10:7). In terms of the Nicene Creed, which makes use of Greek philosophical terminology, God reveals himself through Christ: "He is of one substance [essence] with the Father." Finally, God is in all because by the presence of the Holy Spirit he dwells within his created order. The technical words of theologians to describe the relation of God to the world are transcendence (presence outside the universe), transparence (presence through created objects and beings), and immanence (presence within the universe).

OTHER VIEWS

If people believe and teach that God is only found *in the universe* then they are pantheists (*pan* = all of nature and *theos* = god). Certain philosophers (e.g., B. Spinoza of Amsterdam, a seventeenth-century Jewish thinker) have expounded such a view. Certain English poets, usually called the nature poets, have also come close to pantheism in their views. For example, Wordsworth wrote:

And I have felt
A presence that disturbs me with the joy
Of elevated thoughts: a sense sublime
Of something far more deeply interfused,
Whose swelling is the light of setting suns,
And the round ocean and the living air,

And the blue sky, and in the mind of man;
A motion and a spirit that impels
All thinking things, all objects of all thought,
And rolls through all things.

(Lines composed a few miles above Tintern Abbey)

We reject pantheism, which draws no
distinction between the Creator and what is
created, because it denies that God is outside
and above the world. We also reject the pursuit
of "the divine spark within us," favored by the
devotees of Indian mysticism, for the same
reason.

If people think of God as only being *above the
universe* they also make a mistake. Such a
viewpoint is often called deism and is best
illustrated by the story of the clockmaker and
his clock. He carefully made a clock, wound it
up, and then left it completely alone to tick
away. So, say the deists, God made the world to
run according to the laws of nature which he
had built into the creation. God is totally
separated from the universe he has made.
Christians reject this view because it does not
acknowledge God as existent *through* and *in*
the universe.

When human beings have thought of God as
existing *through the universe* they usually have
been polytheists (*poly* = many; i.e., worshipers
of several gods). The truth underlying
polytheism is that God does manifest himself
through objects and human personalities. But we
reject polytheism because it takes no account
of God as outside and above the world when it

reduces him to merely displaying his existence through finite symbols and persons.

The genuinely Christian thinker is usually called a theist; he claims that in relation to the universe God is transcendent, transparent, and immanent. He is both far and near; he is away from us and yet with us.

Pantheism, deism, and polytheism are views which have been held in different forms by many people over many centuries. In modern times further erroneous views of the relationship of God to the universe have been put forward by philosophers and theologians. One such view is panentheism, and it is related to what is called process theology. The most well-known names associated with this way of thinking are A. N. Whitehead and Charles Hartshorne. It is their belief that the idea of "process" or "becoming" must be applied to both the world and to God. While the traditional Christian theist sees God as perfect and unchangeable, these thinkers and their disciples see in him the supreme example of the capacity for growth and development. As human beings develop through response to others and to the world, so God is in the process of development as he responds to the world, which is included in himself. Thus God is seen as both separate from the world and also involved in the evolution of the world. This way of thinking is a kind of half-way house between theism and pantheism. It identifies God far too closely with the world of process, change, and "becoming" and thus ignores the eternal unchangeableness which the

Bible asserts is an attribute of God (see chapter six).

There is not the space here to go into other modern erroneous views. All that is possible is the naming of them and the provision in the bibliography of books which help the reader to do further study. Two which are fairly popular are those of Paul Tillich and John Macquarrie. The views of Tillich were popularized by Bishop John Robinson in his best-selling book *Honest to God,* and they are often summarized under the heading, God is "the Ground of our being." The views of Macquarrie, outlined in his text-book, *Principles of Christian Theology,* could appear to resemble pantheism. They begin with the experience of man in the world and the philosophy known as existentialism. The definition of God is that of "holy being"—not "a holy being" in some distant sphere. God as "holy being" is closely related to our own being as humans. So Macquarrie calls his theology an "existential-ontological theism."

EVOLUTION AND CREATION

For over a century there has been a continuing debate, sometimes quite heated, concerning the relation of the scientific hypothesis of evolution (which is stated in different ways by scientists) and the biblical account of creation in Genesis 1 (which is interpreted in different ways by theologians). Here we want to suggest that possibly a false perspective of the relation between evolution and creation has led to the questionable assumption that a hypothesis of evolution and a belief in divine creation out of nothing are necessarily opposites. In fact, evolution and creation belong to two different orders of thought. They are not two similar but two different interpretations of the same reality.

If the question is asked, "What is evolution?" the answer must be made in terms of principles (laws) derived from scientific observation and investigation. The laws of science are based on past observations and, consequently, are rational interpretations of what has been observed to be the case. Thus the law that the fittest survive is a description of what appears to happen; it cannot prescribe what must happen in the future. Scientific laws are descriptive and not prescriptive. They do not exist in their own right as a reality but are human deductions from the observation of reality.

To believe that God is the Creator is different. This belief is not a law of science but is given by God's revelation. Genesis 1 contains neither a scientific theory nor a set of scientific laws. It is an inspired statement of faith in which God is proclaimed as the Creator of the whole universe. Likewise, those portions of the New Testament which tell us that God the Son shared with God the Father in creating the world are statements of faith, based on revelation. Thus we believe that in the beginning God made everything "good." This does not mean that the creation was perfect in the sense in which God is perfect. The perfection of the creation lies in the fact that it is the perfect arena in which the will of God is to be fulfilled. The entrance of sin into this good world has not ruined it, but it has certainly made it necessary for God to prepare a new universe which will replace this present one at the end of the present age.

The doctrine of creation clarifies the relationship between God and man. It is through the reality and fact of creation that humanity faces God, for it is within his creation that God reaches toward man. While God is beyond, through, and in the universe, he is still other than the created order and he cannot be identified with it. Man is totally dependent on God at all times and this is true whether he realizes it or not. Adam and Eve were dependent upon God both before they sinned and after they sinned. Today we are dependent upon God not only for our human life but also for our salvation. However, the fact of being created and having God as our Creator does not in any way guarantee our salvation. As will become clear in the next chapter, to receive God's salvation is only possible when we are able (by God's help) to recognize our total dependency on him. We cannot rely upon or trust in any aspect of the created order; we must trust in God alone.

FOUR
God Is Active in Salvation

The evangelist who proclaims the Good News must believe that God is active today or else he would never be an evangelist. He confidently expects the lives of people to be changed by God as they receive the Word of God and become obedient to the Lord. And they are changed. So he can tell of the marvelous changes in both character and life-style of different people in the various places he has worked. By means of such a man's preaching, God the Father is offering God the Son through the power of the Holy Spirit; people respond in the power of the Holy Spirit by receiving the Son who gives eternal life (John 1:12, 13; 17:3).

All Christians believe that God is active in the lives of those who have received the Son and who are continuing in the life of obedience to him. They experience the guidance of the Holy Spirit, and at different times the healing of

71

illnesses and diseases, the preservation from danger, and the provision of necessary blessings. Many personal testimonies could illustrate this point.

Christians also believe that God is active in the history of the peoples of the world. At civic services of worship a nominally Christian nation may thank God for his control of human history and for his blessings to the nation (e.g., at St. Paul's Cathedral, London, on June 7, 1977, British leaders thanked God for his help during the twenty-five years of the reign of Elizabeth II). And, if God is active in the present, Christians also believe he will be active in the future. They don't have to fear that the world will end in confusion through the misuse by men of terrible weapons of war. They believe that God is in control of the future—although knowing this does not mean that they must be inactive for peace in the world.

GOD'S ACTIVITY IN SALVATION

Ever since the ministry of Jesus, God has been active in creating and expanding his Church— the community of people of all races, sexes, and creeds (Gal. 3:28), the Body of Christ (Eph. 4:4, 12), and the Temple of the Holy Spirit (1 Cor. 3:17). The Church is the creation and possession of the Triune Lord; a people who exist for the glory of God by offering spiritual sacrifices through Jesus Christ to God the Father in the power of the Spirit (1 Pet. 2:4).

Sometimes we talk as if the activity of God in

the Church is only the work of the Holy Spirit. Certainly God the Holy Spirit is active in the world, for Jesus himself said: "And when [the Counsellor] comes, he will convince the world concerning sin and righteousness and judgment; concerning sin, because they do not believe in me; concerning righteousness, because I go to the Father, and you will see me no more; concerning judgment, because the ruler of this world is judged" (John 16:8, 10, 11). When he had to deal with the misuse of spiritual gifts in the church at Corinth, Paul wrote to say that "there are varieties of gifts, but the same Spirit; and there are varieties of service, but the same Lord; and there are varieties of working, but it is the same God who inspires them all in every one" (1 Cor. 12:4-6). So the Spirit is active in the Church, but his activity is also the activity of God the Son and God the Father.

There is also a present activity of God the Father and God the Son outside the Church. As sinners repent and believe on the Lord Jesus Christ, God the Father justifies them, adopts them into the family of God, and enrolls their names in heaven (Rom. 5:1-11; 8:1, ff.; Rev. 3:5). God the Son, the exalted Lord who "sits at the right hand of the Father" is active as our heavenly High Priest, Mediator and Advocate, who is ever presenting his work to God and praying for us that our salvation shall be sure and complete (Heb. 7:25; Rom. 8:34). And the Holy Spirit is he who comes to the world and to the churches from the Father and the Son: we affirm in the Nicene Creed that "he proceeds from the Father and the Son and with the Father and the Son is worshiped and glorified," which is teaching based primarily on the Gospel of John.

God does not do or say things haphazardly. His words and actions proceed from perfect thought. As human beings with finite minds, we can only have a partial insight into the mind of God. We can only penetrate as far as God allows us to go. In Paul's letter to the Ephesians we possess an important insight into God's thoughts concerning our salvation.

> Blessed be the God and Father of our Lord Jesus Christ, who has blessed us in Christ with every spiritual blessing in the heavenly places, even as he chose us in him before the foundation of the world, that we should be holy and blameless before him. He destined us in love to be his sons through Jesus Christ, according to the purpose of his will, to the praise of his glorious grace which he freely bestowed on us in the Beloved (Eph. 1:3-6).

The idea of God planning our salvation before he created the world is certainly difficult to understand. Yet we are given such information in Scripture not so that we can speculate about it, but rather to cause us to bow our knees and worship God, who is greater than our greatest thoughts of him (Rom. 11:33-36). However, when this topic is raised there are always those who ask such questions as: "If God made provision for the salvation of the Church before the creation of the world, does this mean that he knew that sin would enter the world and that he was going to do nothing to prevent it?" and, "Does not the idea of God choosing men and women for salvation before the world is created or they are born raise all kinds of problems about God's love for the human race?"

To the first question the only answer which begins to make sense is the following: God made human beings as free agents, free to obey and love him, free also to disobey and hate him. He made them free because he wanted their freely given love, obedience, and worship. Yet, as the Lord who knows the beginning and the end of all things, he knew that human beings would exercise their freedom in such a way as to abuse it. In experimenting with their freedom they would choose to experiment in disobeying God. The moment in which they engaged in this activity they became sinners (Gen. 3). The only way in which God could have prevented this would have been to make human beings as robots; but then they would not have been human beings at all. Therefore, since he knew what would happen, he planned in advance to enter into human history and affairs in order to give mankind a second chance to be his loving, obedient children.

The second question is certainly a difficult one, raising as it does the old problem of predestination. In this complex area of theology the Bible appears to teach apparently contradictory doctrines. It teaches that before creation God chose for himself, out of the whole population of the world, a people to be his special possession and delight (Eph. 1:3-14). It teaches that God loves all mankind and desires that all people should obey the gospel (1 Tim. 2:4; 4:10). It teaches that salvation is not partly God's work and partly man's but rather is God's work from beginning to end and is, therefore, a free gift to man (Eph. 2:1-10). And it also teaches that men and women have a duty when they hear the gospel to repent of their sins and to believe the word of the Lord (Acts 17:30). Total, rational reconciliation of these doctrines is humanly impossible. Yet they are all part of God's revelation of truth. We must trust that in the age to come, when everything will be made clear, that we will understand how they are related to each other. We must resist attempts to lose one or two of these emphases in order to have a tidy theological system.

What is certain and not debatable for Christians is that God was active in the history of Israel and in the life, death, and resurrection of Jesus Christ as he brought salvation into the world. Paul made this very clear in the sermon he preached at Antioch in Pisidia, recorded in Acts 13:16, ff. Men and women who live in time and space exist within history. God acted within history and in recorded time. Though planned and initiated by God outside time and space, salvation was achieved for us within history. So God's saving activity, though having implications which are beyond space and time (for God himself is everlasting), can be located at specific points and in special people in human history; therefore, dates can be given to these events and to people's lives. This biblical emphasis on God entering into time and space to provide salvation for us is found in a developed form only in Christianity.

Judaism, based on the Old Testament, emphasizes God's activity in a lesser degree, while Islam also has some reference to it. In Hinduism and other Eastern religious systems, history is not taken as seriously as a vehicle through which God operates and brings salvation. In these, salvation is salvation *from* history, not *within* history.

In the Old Testament the greatest, but not the only saving event, is the Exodus. While guiding the descendants of Abraham out of Egypt, across the Red Sea and into the deserts of Sinai, God caused his presence to be felt by the freed slaves (Exod. 13—20). The people heard the voice of the Lord coming out of the fire but they could not see him (Deut. 4:15; 5:22). Moses ascended the mountain and received the Law of the Lord (Exod. 19, 20). The people of Israel—the former slaves—entered into a covenant with the Lord (Exod. 24:3-8) and thereby became an elect nation, the chosen people of Yahweh. He was their God and they were his people. These events became the basis for their whole life as a nation and as a worshiping people. The confessions of faith of ancient Israel make this clear. They were recited in Palestine.

> When your son asks you in time to come, "What is the meaning of the testimonies and the statutes and the ordinances which the Lord our God has commanded you?" then you shall say to your son, "We were Pharaoh's slaves in Egypt; and the Lord brought us out of Egypt with a mighty hand; and the Lord showed signs and wonders, great and grievous, against Egypt and against Pharaoh and all his household, before our eyes; and he brought us out from there, that he might bring us in and give us the land which he swore to give to our fathers. And the Lord commanded us to do all these statutes, to fear the Lord our God, for our good always, that he might preserve us alive, as at this day. And it will be righteousness for us, if we are careful to do all this commandment before the Lord our God, as he has commanded us" (Deut. 6:20-25).

There are similar confessions, well worth reading, in Deuteronomy 26:5-9 and in Joshua 24:2-13.

The same theme is found often in the psalms which were sung in the Temple of Jerusalem.

> I will call to mind the deeds of the Lord;
> yea, I will remember thy wonders of old.
> I will meditate on all thy work,
> and muse on thy mighty deeds.

Thy way, O God, is holy,
What god is great like our God?
Thou art the God who workest wonders,
who hast manifested thy might among the
peoples.
Thou didst with thy arm redeem thy people,
the sons of Jacob and Joseph (Psa. 77:11-15).

Again it is well worth reading further psalms—
78, 105, and 136 for example.

In the New Testament God is seen as active
in bringing salvation into the world through the
incarnate Son of God, especially through his
saving death and resurrection. These events are
even portrayed as a second and greater Exodus.
While the first Exodus preceded the creation of
the Mosaic Covenant, the second Exodus in
Christ preceded the new covenant. Prophets of
the old covenant spoke of the new covenant
(Jer. 31:31, ff.; Ezek. 36:24-28). Words which
are used in the Old Testament to describe the
nature of the work of God in the first Exodus
are used by the New Testament writers to
describe the work of God in the greater, second
Exodus—words like redemption, deliverance,
ransom, purchase, and freedom. Jesus himself
said that he did not come to be ministered unto
but rather to minister to others and to give
his life as a ransom for many (Mark 10:45).

When Zechariah, father of John the Baptist,
spoke of the birth of John and his mission in
the world he knew that God was beginning a
mighty work:

Blessed be the Lord God of Israel,
for he has visited and redeemed his people,
and has raised up a horn of salvation for us,
in the house of his servant David
    (Luke 1:68, 69).

And when the devout Simeon held the baby
Jesus in the Temple he expressed his readiness
to die, with his hopes now realized,

for mine eyes have seen thy salvation
which thou hast prepared in the presence of
    all peoples,
a light for revelation to the Gentiles,
and for glory to thy people Israel
    (Luke 2:30-32).

At the close of his ministry as the Jewish
Messiah, Jesus kept the feast of the Passover
with his disciples in Jerusalem. In doing this he
instituted what we call the Lord's Supper. The
broken bread symbolized his body, given as a
sacrifice for our sins; and the wine symbolized
his blood, poured out for us in order that we
might be brought to God (Luke 22:14-20). Thus
by his death and resurrection, proclaimed by
churches each time they keep the Lord's Supper,
Jesus Christ began the second, great Exodus. As
the Israelites were in bondage to Pharaoh, so
human beings are in bondage to sin. They are
slaves of sin (Rom. 6:14, ff.). Christ set his people
free from the bondage of hell and sin; he set
them on the way to the promised land of joy and
peace in the Holy Spirit in this life and in the life

to come. So when we are baptized, we are baptized into the death of Jesus in order that dying to sin we might rise to newness of life in him (Rom. 6:1-11). What Christ did for us is well summarized by Paul who wrote, "He has delivered us from the dominion of darkness and transferred us to the kingdom of his beloved Son, in whom we have redemption, the forgiveness of sins" (Col. 1:13, 14). Also, in the words from his Epistle to the Ephesians: ". . . Christ loved the Church and gave himself up for her, that he might sanctify her, having cleansed her by the washing of water with the word, that he might present the Church to himself in splendor, without spot or wrinkle or any such thing, that she might be holy and without blemish" (Eph. 5:25-27).

So we see that God's activity in providing salvation is accomplished in history through mighty acts and supremely through the death and resurrection of Christ; it is also appropriated and received by those who live within time and history. We receive salvation in time and history so that we can by God's grace enjoy eternal life with him, first in history, and then outside time and space as we now know them. And salvation for the Christian is primarily a new relationship with God the Father, through the Son, in the power of the Spirit. It is at this point that the Christian faith differs from Hinduism and those religions and sects which are associated with it. The Hindu hopes for the release of his soul from his body in order that it might be absorbed into Brahman; this is escape from history. The devotions and exercises associated with Yoga have a similar significance since in Yoga the devotee seeks to lose his human, worldly consciousness in order to find another level of consciousness and be lost in that. Salvation here is *from* time and history, whereas for Christianity it is *in* and through time and history.

GOD'S ACTIVITY IN GUIDING AND CONTROLLING HISTORY

We have been emphasizing the fact that God brought salvation into the world through historical events and people. The Bible also teaches that God is in control of all history, for he is the sovereign Lord of all. It was the conviction of Israel that all aspects of its history, its triumphs and failures, its journeyings and sojournings, were directly controlled by God. He was with them in battles; "Hear, O Israel, you draw near this day to battle against your enemies: let not your heart faint; do not fear, or tremble, or be in dread of them; for the Lord your God is he that goes with you, to fight for you against your enemies, to give you the victory" (Deut. 20:3, 4). But if they turned from him to worship the gods of Canaan then they were in trouble. "They forsook the Lord, and served the Baals and the Ashtaroth. So the anger of the Lord was kindled against Israel, and he gave them over to plunderers, who plundered them; and he sold them into the power of their enemies round about, so that they could no

82

longer withstand their enemies" (Judg. 2:13, 14).

The kingship of Yahweh over all nations is seen when he makes use of the great empires of the ancient world in order to punish or help, as the case may be, the people of Israel. Speaking through Isaiah, God referred to the great empire of Assyria in the following terms: "Ah, Assyria, the rod of my anger, the staff of my fury! Against a godless nation I send him, and against the people of my wrath I command him" (Isa. 10:5, 6). Later, of the Persian Empire and its king, Cyrus, God said: "Thus says the Lord to his anointed, to Cyrus, whose right hand I have grasped, to subdue nations before him and ungird the loins of kings, to open doors before him that gates may not be closed" (Isa. 45:1, 2).

A constant theme in the Psalms is "the Lord reigns" (Psa. 96:10; 97:1; 99:1) and "God reigns over the nations" (Psa. 47:8). As Creator, Yahweh is Lord and King of the whole world and he judges the nations in righteousness.

The Lord reigns; let the peoples tremble!
He sits enthroned upon the cherubim; let
    the earth quake!
The Lord is great in Zion;
he is exalted over all the peoples (Psa. 99:1, 2).

For the Lord is a great God,
and a great King above all gods.
In his hand are the depths of the earth;
the heights of the mountains are his also.
The sea is his, for he made it;
for his hands formed the dry land (Psa. 95:3-5).

In the words of the prophet, Daniel, God "the Most High rules the kingdom of men and gives it to whom he will" (Dan. 4:32).

Isaiah was so sure that only Yahweh reigned and that the gods of the other nations were but idols of stone, metal, or wood, that he challenged the idols and nations to show their power:

> Set forth your case, says the Lord;
> bring your proofs, says the King of Jacob.
> Let them bring them, and tell us what is to
>   happen.
> Tell us the former things, what they are,
> that we may consider them,
> that we may know their outcome;
> or declare to us the things to come.
> Tell us what is to come hereafter,
> that we may know that you are gods;
> do good, or do harm,
> that we may be dismayed and terrified.
> Behold, you are nothing,
> and your work is nought;
> an abomination is he who chooses you
>   (Isa. 41:21-24).

Thus for prophets and priests, for kings and people, Yahweh was the *King*. As King he ruled over all the human kings of the earth.

In the New Testament the same viewpoint is presumed and adopted. It was not at any random moment in history but "when the time had fully come, God sent forth his Son, born of woman" (Gal. 4:4). It was providential that at the time when Jesus founded his Church there were: the "Roman peace," bringing stability to the Mediterranean lands; the Roman roads, making travel comparatively easy; and the universally used Greek language, making communication possible.

The writers of the New Testament attribute the rule of world history to both the Father and the Son, while the Holy Spirit is seen as active in the outworking of this control. God the Father is the One from whom all human authority and government is derived: "For there is no authority except from God, and those that exist have been instituted by God" (Rom. 13:1). From heaven John heard the voice of a multitude who cried, "Hallelujah! For the Lord our God the Almighty reigns" (Rev. 19:6). After his resurrection Jesus claimed: "All authority in heaven and on earth has been given to me" (Matt. 28:18). In the last book of the Bible he is called "Lord of lords and King of kings" (Rev. 17:14; 19:16).

Today some Christians claim that the most obvious evidence that God is the Lord of the nations is to be found in the foundation and progress of the nation-state of Israel within the last three decades. The fact that physical descendants of the Jews of biblical times are now living in Palestine is taken to be a direct fulfillment of certain prophecies of the Old Testament. Some words of caution are necessary here. In the period in which we now live, the evidence of God's rule over history is much more difficult to understand, assess, and interpret than it was when all God's elect people were in

one nation-state (as in Old Testament times).
God's rule of the nations is according to his own
secret will, and though we know it is for his
glory and for the final good of his people, we
cannot know the totality or even minor details
of God's mind in this regard.

The point is simply this: all Christians should
believe that God is the Lord of the nations and
is ruling them according to his own will. This
knowledge gives them peace of mind when
human affairs seem hopelessly corrupt or
fragile. But we do not know the secrets of God's
will; therefore, we must not speculate as to
how and why specific nations rise and fall.

We must await our entry into the age to come
when, in the fullness of the divine blessing,
these matters will be made clear to us.
Meanwhile, we follow the example of those
described in the book of Revelation and offer
ceaseless worship to the Lord who reigns.

GOD'S ACTIVITY IN MAKING A NEW CREATION

In the last chapter we considered God's activity
in creation. In this chapter our primary concern
has been with the activity of God in salvation.
We now have the opportunity to combine these
two themes by discussing the new creation
which God is preparing.

In the Bible the creation is presented as the
first of God's saving works (Isa. 44:21-28;
51:12-16). God, having created, does not stand
back in isolation from the creation but he
sustains it and saves people within it. In this

process of salvation, he is active making a new order of people and a new order of existence in which they will live. Christ is the Second Adam, the head of a new humanity, and for him and his people, a new heaven and earth are being prepared (Rom. 5:12-21); the old creation in which we live knows that this is to be and so it groans in expectation of it (Rom. 8:20-23).

The "new creation" is the result of the living response of men and women to the saving word of the gospel which comes in the power of the Holy Spirit. God preaches his Word, the Lord Jesus Christ, to man; and in man, the new creation is formed as he responds to the gospel. Becoming a new creation is not just a matter of personal reorientation toward God. It is God remaking a man to live for God. In this work of making a new creation God is reaching into our earthbound relationships and into ourselves as people in order to begin to transform us and fit us for the life he has planned for us.

The problem with writing anything precise about the "new creation" is that one has to take account of human limitations and the perfection of God at the same time. This would be an impossible task if it were not for the One who was himself fully God and fully man, the incarnate Son of God, Jesus Christ. The new creation finds its fullest expression in Jesus Christ; Christians are part of the new creation in him. To be part of the new creation is to become part of God's activity as Creator and Savior. This activity is accomplished within us by the power of the Holy Spirit who is molding us and fashioning us after the pattern of Christ.

In the book of Revelation, in John's vision of the end of this age, the One who is the "beginning and the end" sends down the New Jerusalem (Rev. 21:2). At the end, all things are completed in him and God becomes all in all (1 Cor. 15:28). The imagery in which John records his vision bridges the gap between what is temporal and what is everlasting. At the center of the imagery stands Jesus Christ the Lamb who is worthy "to receive power and wealth and wisdom and might and honor and glory and blessing" (Rev. 5:12). The Lamb is described as being in the midst of God's throne (5:6). Such imagery is an emphatic reversal of the normal picture of the shepherd tending his lambs and leading a flock of sheep to new pastures. Now the Lamb acts as the shepherd and leads the new flock (the new humanity) to living pastures and living water. This action of the Lamb is God's activity in the new creation.

FIVE
God Is Powerful

The word "power" is often in the vocabulary of the committed Christian. He prays for "power from on high," he refers to the "power of prayer," he claims that "there is wonder-working power in the blood of Calvary," and he states that with God all things are possible. All these suggest that basic to Christianity is the belief that God is omnipotent or all-powerful. And the widespread influence of the charismatic movement has increased the awareness of Christians of God's power to heal. In this chapter we shall show that the activity of God in creating, upholding, and guiding the universe, as well as in guiding history and bringing salvation, is the activity of the omnipotent Lord.

THE POWER OF GOD AS PORTRAYED IN THE OLD TESTAMENT

When God made himself known to Abram he said to him, "I am God Almighty; walk before me, and be blameless" (Gen. 17:1). Many years later the word of the Lord came to Jeremiah: "Behold, I am the Lord, the God of all flesh; is anything too hard for me?" (Jer. 32:27). Obviously, God expected the answer "No."

Behind the great act of creating the world is the power of God and the power of his word. Jeremiah wrote that "It is he who made the earth by his power" (Jer. 10:12), and through him God said: "It is I who by my great power and my outstretched arm have made the earth" (Jer. 27:5). The psalmist sang:

Let all the earth fear the Lord,
let all the inhabitants of the world stand in
     awe of him!
For he spoke, and it came to be;
he commanded, and it stood forth
     (Psa. 33:8, 9).

By the same powerful commands the Lord also maintains his universe.

Behind each miracle from the Exodus to the fall of Jericho was the power of God. Let us look at one example in Numbers 11. In the deserts of Sinai the people of Israel moaned to Moses because they had not had sufficient meat to eat. Moses prayed to the Lord, who answered: "Is the Lord's hand shortened?" By means of this anthropomorphism the Lord was telling Moses that he had just as much strength as he ever had. And he proved it by causing thousands of quails to be blown into the deserts of Sinai and to fall exhausted near the camps of Israel. He also proved it by punishing with death those Israelites who had craved for meat instead of being satisfied with God's provision of manna.

The almighty power of God was a source for worship:

Be exalted, O Lord, in thy strength!
We will sing and praise thy power (Psa. 21:13).

But I will sing of thy might;
I will sing aloud of thy steadfast love in the
    morning (Psa. 59:16).

His omnipotence was to be proclaimed to others:

Come and see what God has done:
he is terrible in his deeds among men.
He turned the sea into dry land;
men passed through the river on foot.
There did we rejoice in him,
who rules by his might for ever (Psa. 66:5-7).

Yet he saved them for his name's sake,
that he might make known his mighty power.
He rebuked the Red Sea, and it became dry;
and he led them through the deep as through
    a desert (Psa. 106:8, 9).

It was also a basis for private meditation:

On the glorious splendor of thy majesty,
and on thy wondrous works, I will meditate
    (Psa. 145:5).

The active God is the powerful God.

For the Israelite to think of God as almighty was to think of God exercising his power in two ways. First, power meant authority and Yahweh was the King of the nations. Second, power meant strength, strength many times greater than that of a strong man such as Samson. This power made the world and performed the miracles.

THE POWER OF GOD AS
PORTRAYED IN THE NEW TESTAMENT

The writers of the New Testament accept the teaching of the Old Testament that God is omnipotent and that his power was the cause of creation and of the great miracles (Acts 17:24). For them the power of God was particularly seen in the power of the Messiah, of the Holy Spirit, and of the gospel.

Jesus Christ, the Savior, possessed the authority and power of God. He told his disciples: "All authority in heaven and on earth has been given to me" (Matt. 28:18). Before his death and resurrection he revealed the power of God in the way that he dealt with evil spirits. He cast them out of people and also gave power to his disciples to cast them out (Mark 5:1, ff.; 6:7; Luke 9:1). He also had power over sickness and illness of every kind and so was able to heal people and to give his disciples power to heal (Luke 8:40, ff.; 9:1, 2). He also showed that he had power over the universe in his provision of sufficient bread for the crowds (Mark 6:30, ff.), in his stilling of the storm (Mark 4:35, ff.), and in his walking on the water (Mark 6:48, ff.).

He also demonstrated that he had power over death. When Lazarus was dead he called him back to life (John 12). Likewise, he gave life to the dead son of the widow of Nain (Luke 7:11, ff.), and to the daughter of Jairus (Mark 5:22, ff.). In his own resurrection God's power was supremely illustrated (John 10:18; Rom. 1:2-4).

After his resurrection and ascension the exalted Jesus sent the Holy Spirit to his Church and the Spirit brought the power of the Lord to the Lord's people. "But you shall receive power when the Holy Spirit has come upon you," said Jesus (Acts 1:8). In the power of the Spirit the apostles preached, evangelized, and healed the sick. The power of God is contained in the gospel so that the effects of receiving the gospel involve a mighty change in the destiny of those who receive it. Paul declared that he was not ashamed of the gospel for "it is the power of God for salvation to every one who has faith" (Rom. 1:16). This power of God which makes conversions possible (Eph. 1:19) is the same power which, at the end of the age, will bring into being our new resurrection bodies (Phil. 3:10; 1 Cor. 15:12, ff.). It is also the same power which enables the believer to triumph over sin and temptation in this present life (Rom. 8:1-8; 15:13).

Out of his love and wisdom God devised and made possible our salvation. Now by his great power he brings that salvation into our lives and into our world. The only limits to the almighty

93

power of God are those which his own wisdom sets. Did not Jesus say that "with God all things are possible" (Matt. 19:26)? God is always almighty and omnipotent.

MIRACLES TODAY

The fact that God does not change will be discussed in the next chapter. The power which he has displayed in creation, in the great Exodus from Egypt to Canaan, and in the resurrection of Jesus, is the power which he possesses today. As we ponder the immensity and complexity of the universe in which we live we often admit to ourselves and perhaps tell others that "it is a miracle that it continues in such an orderly manner." The hymn writer, Isaac Watts, expressed for Christians this response:

I sing the almighty power of God,
That made the mountains rise,
That spread the flowing seas abroad,
And built the lofty skies.

But what do we mean by "miracle"?

We use the term in different ways. It can mean that which is normally impossible for human beings to achieve. For example, if a brilliant scientist actually made a beetle which lived and could fly then we would say this was a miracle. It would qualify since, as far as we know, the total scientific expertise available today could not give life to an insect. The word miracle is also used in a more technical sense, to refer to the suspension, or bypassing, by God of what we call the laws of nature. So the raising of the dead by Jesus or the amazing cure of a person with an advanced cancer today are miracles. Since God made everything, including the laws of nature, we must believe that he is at perfect liberty to perform what we call miracles whenever it pleases him to do so. To people who have a strong belief that God, the Lord, is the Creator and Sustainer of his universe, the fact that God sometimes apparently contravenes his own laws is not a major problem. For what we call "laws" are based on our observations, and God is not bound by these.

Why then, it is often asked, are there not more miracles today? Why are not more people healed of their sicknesses? It would seem that since God is all-powerful and loving there should be, alongside the conversion of sinners to Christ, more obvious manifestations of the power of God in miracles. We read that Jesus "healed many who were sick with various diseases, and cast out many demons" (Mark 1:34) and that "many wonders and signs were done through the apostles" (Acts 2:43).

Today, the actual, observable facts appear to be that while there are some genuine miracles (especially of healing), these tend to be the exception rather than the rule. At special services of healing, in evangelistic campaigns, in the ministry and fellowship of the local church, and at the personal level, the number actually healed seems to be only a proportion of those for whom prayer for healing is offered.

Certainly the living Lord sometimes intervenes in the normal processes of the universe and of human life in order to heal his people. But most of us still feel that these occasions are not quite so plentiful as we would wish. We think of the teaching of Jesus concerning faith which can move mountains (Mark 11:23-25). We also remember the words of Jesus: "Truly, truly, I say to you, he who believes in me will also do the works that I do; and greater works than these will he do, because I go to the Father. Whatever you ask in my name, I will do it, that the Father may be glorified in the Son; if you ask anything in my name, I will do it" (John 14:12, 13).

Kathryn Kuhlman, whom God used as a minister of healing on many occasions, often asked herself why some people were healed in her services and others were not. Toward the end of her life she wrote: "Now I see that we can't demand or command that God do anything. In general, I definitely believe that it is God's will to heal. But I can't say absolutely what is or is not his will in a particular case. There are some things I've learned just not to touch" (A. Spraggett, *Kathryn Kuhlman, The Woman Who Believes in Miracles*, 1970, quoted by F. MacNutt, *Healing*, 1974, p. 147.).

It is possible, of course, that the words of Jesus quoted above from John 14 were intended to describe the ministry of the apostles in their unique work of laying the foundation of the Christian Church (Eph. 2:20). Certainly the majority of the miracles described in Scripture are an integral part of the revelation of God to man. The supply of manna to the Israelites was part of the great saving event of the Exodus (Exod. 16:15, 31). The healing of Naaman, the commander of the king of Aram's army, was part of the revelation to people outside the nation of Israel that Yahweh is the living Lord (2 Kgs. 5:7, 14). The miracles of Jesus are closely linked to his mission and work as the long expected Jewish Messiah (Luke 4:16, ff.), while those of the apostles are part of the actual work of the Holy Spirit in establishing the Church according to prophecy (Acts 2:14, ff. citing Joel 2:28, ff.). This does not mean that God did not work any miracles after the death of the last apostle. Certainly he did work miracles in the early centuries of the history of the Church just as he does today. But we must interpret Scripture with care in terms of making deductions as to what we can rightfully expect today from the power and love of God.

In his book, *Healing*, Francis MacNutt rightly makes the point that for the most part we need encouragement to believe that God *does* heal people. However, he feels it necessary to devote chapter 18 to the topic "Eleven reasons why people are not healed." These are: (1) lack of faith in Christians; (2) God is using the sickness for a higher purpose; e.g., to promote holiness; (3) people are conditioned to think that God has sent the suffering as a chastisement; (4) the sickness is closely connected with a sin which has not been forsaken; (5) there has been no specific prayer for healing; (6) there has been the wrong type of prayer; e.g., prayer for deliverance from an evil spirit rather than prayer for inner, spiritual healing; (7) there has been a refusal to use ordinary medicine as one way in which God heals; (8) care has not been taken to obey obvious rules for good health; (9) God's time to heal is not yet come; (10) a different person or means is to be the way God will send healing; and (11) the social environment prevents healing from taking place.

Like the problem of evil and suffering, to which we turn in chapter seven, the reason why miracles sometimes occur and sometimes do not occur is in the last analysis a mystery. It belongs to the wisdom of God into which we do not have full access in this mortal life.

SIX
God Is Unchanging

One obvious fact about human beings is that they change. They grow from being babies to children, from children to young adults, and then from adults to old people. Though there is a continuity of identity, their size and appearance change. So also do their ideas, views, tastes, preferences, and prejudices. In fact everything about us undergoes change, gradually if not rapidly. Even those things around us which appear never to change, the mountains for example, are never exactly the same each moment, for chemical changes are taking place.

Although we have no direct experience of unchangeableness we do nevertheless live out out Christian lives and offer our prayers and worship on the assumption that God never changes in his attitude toward us. We presume that his character and his relationship with us is constant.

Change and decay in all around I see
O Thou who changest not abide with me.

and,

We blossom and flourish as leaves on the tree,
And wither and perish but nought changeth
Thee.

but,

Great is Thy faithfulness, O God my Father,
There is no shadow of turning with Thee.

Since our present Christian experience, as well
as the experience of those who have gone before
and those who will follow after us, is totally
dependent upon God remaining always the same
in himself and toward us, let us note how God is
portrayed in the Bible in his unchanging
character, or, as the theologians express it, in
his *immutability*.

GOD IS ALWAYS IN TRINITY

Some people believe that God only had a Son
from the time of the baptism of Jesus. They
misunderstand the words from heaven: "This is
my beloved son with whom I am well pleased"
(Matt. 3:17). Here Jesus is being confirmed as
the incarnate Son, not being adopted as a Son.
It has been the conviction of the Church over

the centuries that he is the "only Son of God, eternally begotten of the Father, God from God, Light from Light, true God from true God, begotten not made, one in Being with the Father" (Nicene Creed).

The Holy Spirit is the eternal Spirit (Heb. 9:14) who is "the Lord, the giver of life, who proceeds from the Father and the Son. With the Father and the Son he is worshiped and glorified" (Nicene Creed). The Father is certainly also eternal. He is "the Father of lights with whom there is no variation or shadow due to change" (Jas. 1:17). He is "the Father, the Almighty, maker of heaven and earth, of all that is seen and unseen" (Nicene Creed).

God—Father, Son, and Holy Spirit—cannot change for he is already perfect, and, being perfect, he cannot change. God alone possesses immortality: he is "the blessed and only Sovereign, the King of kings and Lord of lords, who alone has immortality and dwells in unapproachable light, whom no man has ever seen or can see" (1 Tim. 6:15, 16). He is the first and the last: "Hearken to me, O Jacob, and Israel, whom I have called! I am He, I am the first, and I am the last" (Isa. 48:12).

This theme of God's immutability is expressed rather beautifully in the Psalms:

thy throne is established from of old;
thou art from everlasting (Psa. 93:2).

Before the mountains were brought forth,
or ever thou hadst formed the earth and the
world,
from everlasting to everlasting thou art God
(Psa. 90:2).

Of old thou didst lay the foundation of the
earth,
and the heavens are the work of thy hands.
They will perish, but thou dost endure;
they will all wear out like a garment.
Thou changest them like a raiment,
and they pass away;
but thou art the same, and thy years have no
end.
The children of thy servants shall dwell
secure;
their posterity shall be established before thee
(Psa. 102:25-28).

Again we find the anthropormorphisms here, but
they are inescapable when we try to use our
human language to describe the Lord who is both
infinite and eternal. Indeed, when speaking of
the unchanging triune God we are constantly
having to use a variety of images.

GOD IS ALWAYS HOLY

In a famous book, *The Idea of the Holy*, Rudolf
Otto has shown that in all religions people
relate to what they regard as "the holy." With
appropriate reverence or fear they feel attracted

by whatever seems to be other than themselves and other than their normal day to day experience. The "holy" is the "wholly other."

An illustration may help to convey the attitude people adopt toward "the holy." Think of a great fire—in a forest or a large building. People find that they are both attracted to and repelled by the fire. The marvelous sight of flames rising into the air attracts them but the heat drives them back. So in religious experience all over the world the idea of "the holy" and the "wholly other" both attracts and repels.

In God's disclosure of himself to Israel the note of holiness is central. The Lord who reveals himself is the Holy One. For Israel, the "Wholly Other" is personal; he is Yahweh. Thus in the Bible reverence is toward a holy Person, the living God himself. Our holy God both draws us to himself (for he is holy love), and also repels us because of our sin (for he is pure light).

What the holiness of Yahweh meant for Israel is best seen through the study of several significant Old Testament passages. Let us look, first of all, at the story of Moses and the burning bush (Exod. 3). Moses saw a bush burning brightly and as he approached it a heavenly voice told him not to come too close, for he was standing on sacred soil. Obeying the voice, Moses came to understand that the voice belonged to the God of his fathers. Then Moses "hid his face, for he was afraid to look at God." God was experienced in this incident by Moses as holy—the wholly Other—whom Moses could neither see nor touch. Yet at the same time, Moses was called to serve this holy Lord.

The next passage is Exodus 19. The tribes of Israel gathered near to the mountain on which God intended to communicate with Moses, their leader. In order to teach the people that he was holy, Yahweh required that none of the people were to touch the mountain. It carried, as it were, a high electric charge and for them to touch it would mean death. Then to help them recognize what his holiness meant he caused thunder and lightning to occur above the mountain. This was so severe that the people trembled. Their God was the Holy One but yet, as the rest of the book of Exodus shows, he still called the people into a living relationship with himself.

God's holy presence was not confined to Mount Sinai. It was also attached to the symbol of his presence—the ark of the covenant. In 1 Samuel 6 and 2 Samuel 6 the fate of those who did not recognize the holiness of God, symbolized by the ark, is described, and it is a sad story. Seeing the ark being returned by the Philistines, who had captured it, certain Israelites dared to look into it and seventy of them perished. The villagers who survived said: "Who is able to stand before the Lord, this holy God?" On a later occasion Uzzah accidentally touched the ark when the oxen, who were pulling the cart on which it was placed, stumbled. Though innocent, he perished (2 Sam. 6:6, ff.). Yahweh, it seems, had to teach his people that he truly was holy.

For the most powerful presentation of the holiness of Yahweh we turn to the call of Isaiah, recorded in chapter six of his prophecies. He saw the angels calling one to the other and saying: "Holy, holy, holy is the Lord of hosts; the whole earth is full of his glory." Here holiness is not only the wholly otherness of God, it is also his total perfection and purity. He is separated from space and time; he is also separated from sin. So Isaiah had to confess, "Woe is me! . . . for I am a man of unclean lips." An amazing truth which this vision conveys is that this holy, pure Lord, who is totally separated from all uncleanness, does become involved in his sinful creation. "The whole earth is full of his glory."

Isaiah was to preach God's word to the people of Israel. When he came to deliver his message he described the giver of the word as "the Holy One of Israel" (e.g., Isa. 1:4; 5:19, 24; 10:20; 30:11, 12, 15; 31:1). In the later chapters of the book, "the Holy One of Israel" is portrayed as the Redeemer and Savior of the people. "I will help you, says the Lord; your Redeemer is the Holy One of Israel" (Isa. 41:14); "I am the Lord your God, the Holy One of Israel, your Savior" (Isa. 43:3).

This definite association of holiness with love and mercy reaches its clearest presentation in the Old Testament in the experience and prophecies of Hosea. By means of his experience as the husband of an unfaithful wife he learned about God's hatred of sin and love for sinners. The tension between holiness which must

destroy sin and mercy, which works for the
benefit of sinners, is conveyed by the following
words in which God is speaking:

> I will not execute my fierce anger,
> I will not again destroy Ephraim;
> for I am God and not man,
> the Holy One in your midst,
> and I will not come to destroy (Hos. 11:9).

It is only in the New Testament that God's
nature of *holy love* is fully declared.

Before turning to the New Testament, there
are other aspects of the theme of holiness which
must be noticed. Everything connected with
the Holy One becomes holy by association. God
extends his holy arm (Isa. 52:10); he speaks his
holy word (Psa. 105:42; Jer. 23:9); he is worshiped
on a holy mountain (Isa. 11:9), by a holy nation
(Exod. 19:6; Isa. 62:12), in a holy place (2 Chron.
3:8), with the help of holy priests (Lev. 21:6, 7),
holy Levites (2 Chron. 35:3), and holy prophets
(2 Kgs. 4:9).

It is only against the background of his
holiness that it is possible to appreciate God as
a jealous God. In the Ten Commandments he is
described as a jealous God (Exod. 20:5) and later
the people of Israel are commanded: "you shall
worship no other god, for the Lord, whose name
is Jealous, is a jealous God" (Exod. 34:14). On a
further occasion the people were told that "the
Lord your God is a devouring fire, a jealous God"
(Deut. 4:24). So we see that God is absolutely
intolerant in the sense that he will not permit

worship and service, which is due to him as Lord, to be given to another. We may add here that the wrath of God is also related to his holiness and to his jealousy. He is angry when human beings behave toward him as if he were not the Holy One (see Zeph. 3:8 and Nahum 1:2). Yet there is a positive side to the jealousy of God. He has a passionate zeal for the well-being of his covenant people. So the prophecy from Isaiah describing the future king and savior (Isa. 9:2-7), whom we know to have been Jesus Christ, ends with the words: "The zeal of the Lord of hosts will do this."

In the New Testament the holiness of God is taken for granted. The song of the seraphim heard by Isaiah was also heard by John as he had visions on Patmos. The four living creatures never ceased to sing by day and night:

Holy, holy, holy, is the Lord God Almighty, who was and is and is to come (Rev. 4:8).

Jesus prayed to God as "holy Father" (John 17:11) and he taught his disciples to hallow the name of God (Matt. 6:9). Peter combined the idea of God's holiness with the call to God's people to be holy when he wrote: "but as he who called you is holy, be holy yourselves in all your conduct" (1 Pet. 1:15).

On a few occasions Jesus is described as "the Holy One of God," as in the significant confession of faith made by Simon Peter (John 6:69). In Revelation Jesus is called "the holy one, the true one" (Rev. 3:7), an expression used of

God the Father later (Rev. 6:10). The Spirit of God is the "Holy Spirit" (see Eph. 1:13; 4:30; 1 Thess. 4:8).

And as in the Old Testament, so in the New Testament, those people and things which are closely related to the Holy One are also called holy. The Church is holy (Eph. 5:27), and individual Christians are saints (or, being made holy; see Rom. 12:1; 15:16). In her language the Christian Church has called baptism "holy baptism" and the Lord's Supper "Holy Communion" because of their close ties with the Holy One.

Before we conclude this section on God's holiness we need to look quickly at two further words which convey the same basic ideas. They are "glory" and "light." Yahweh is the "King of glory" (Psa. 24:7-10) and "the glory of Israel" (Mic. 1:15). When he gave the Law to Moses his glory rested on Mount Sinai (Exod. 24:16). At the dedication of the Temple in Jerusalem "the glory of the Lord filled the house" (2 Chron. 5:14). To the psalmist the heavens declared the glory of God (Psa. 19:1), and in his vision Isaiah became conscious that the whole earth is full of God's glory (Isa. 6:3).

Behind these expressions is a simple idea. Israelites believed that the character and personality of a man was revealed by his dress and possessions, which were his glory. God's glory is the manifestation of his presence and of his holiness. God's character of holiness is revealed by the whole world which he has made, or by aspects of the world he has made (smoke, thunder, lightning, etc.). As the glory of the rich man is seen in the abundance of his possessions, so the glory of God is seen in the whole universe.

The glory of the Lord is also seen in his deeds, in what he does for Israel (Psa. 111:2). In the New Testament the glory of God is seen in Jesus Christ. "And the Word became flesh and dwelt among us, full of grace and truth; we have beheld his glory, glory as of the only Son from the Father" (John 1:14). This glory was very apparent to those few disciples who witnessed his transfiguration (Matt. 17:1-8). The glory of God is also seen in the deeds of Jesus Christ, especially in his death, resurrection, and ascension (John 12:23, ff.; 13:31, 32). The experience of Jesus, the Christ, makes it clear that God glorifies himself not at the expense of men, but for their good. God's glory and holiness revealed in Jesus are the salvation of mankind. So Christians are people who recognize and honor God in the excellence (glory) which he shows in his redeeming acts of love. They honor him in obedient living and in hallowing his name. And they look forward to sharing his glory.

"The Lord is my light" (Psa. 27:1) said the psalmist, who lived in the light of, and by the light of, God's revealed will (Law). The Law of Moses revealed God's character of holiness. Moses declared that "the Lord your God is a devouring fire, a jealous God" (Deut. 4:24). This is the negative side of light. God must always be opposed to sin; this is his nature. In the New Testament these images of light and fire are also used. "God is light and in him is no darkness at all" (1 John 1:5). On the Day of Pentecost the descent of the Holy Spirit upon the waiting disciples is described as being like "tongues of fire" (Acts 2:3). The Holy Spirit cleanses our hearts from sin and thus his work is like that of a fire which destroys impurities.

Holiness, then, applies to everything that is God. So he is *Holy* Trinity. He possesses and shows *holy* love, *holy* righteousness, and *holy* justice. He is light and a consuming fire. Holiness is not easy to define. At least it means that God's nature and being are such that when people truly encounter him (in worship, prayer, vision, etc.) they are filled with a sense of awe and reverence; they are overwhelmed by his excellence and purity and their sinfulness. His holy fire drives them away but his holy love, through Christ, draws them close.

GOD IS ALWAYS RIGHTEOUS

God's righteousness is unchanging in that God's dealings with mankind are always right. His law governing the behavior of mankind is just. The psalmist wrote: "I will praise thee with an upright heart, when I learn thy righteous ordinances" (Psa. 119:7).

In the Old Testament we find that God's righteousness is God himself in action as he relates to and deals with the Israelites or their neighbors. His dealings are always according to his own perfect moral standards. Therefore, his righteousness can in one case bring salvation to a people or a person whereas in another it can

110

bring judgment and punishment. Psalm 85 closes with a joyful affirmation of the righteousness of God: "Yea, the Lord will give what is good, and our land will yield its increase. Righteousness will go before him, and make his footsteps a way." Psalm 89 celebrates the righteousness of God: "Righteousness and justice are the foundation of thy throne; steadfast love and faithfulness go before thee" (v. 14). The righteous God expects his people to be righteous. In their dealings with him they are to do right, that is to trust and obey him.

Righteousness is given in full measure to the Messiah who will establish and uphold his Kingdom "with justice and with righteousness" (Isa. 9:7). Through Jeremiah the word of the Lord was declared: "Behold the days are coming, says the Lord, when I will raise up for David a righteous Branch, and he shall reign as king and deal wisely, and shall execute justice and righteousness in the land" (Jer. 23:5).

The righteousness of God works naturally, and in the first place in favor of Israel in general and the pious Israelites in particular. It does, however, work among all the nations (Psa. 9:8) for Yahweh is judge over all peoples and is Lord over the whole world (Psa. 99) which he judges righteously (Psa. 98:9).

God's righteousness is a reality which the religious man does not question. "Righteous art thou, O Lord, when I complain to thee," said Jeremiah (12:1). Job had his belief in God's righteousness fully tested, but in the end his conviction had not changed (see Job 23:8-17, ff.).

In the New Testament the word righteousness, when used of human beings, means living in a right relationship with God. We are to serve God "without fear, in holiness and righteousness before him all the days of our life" (Luke 1:75). Our righteousness is to exceed that of the scribes and Pharisees (Matt. 5:20). In fact, the righteousness which God demands we can never of ourselves supply. But he provides what he demands in Jesus Christ. Thus the term righteousness, when used of God, refers to his activity through Jesus Christ of giving to men the gift of righteousness (Rom. 1:17; 3:21-28).

Righteousness is a dynamic property of God which is active in the world as he justifies men and women by reckoning to them the righteousness of Christ. So the word righteousness can be understood either as divine activity, or the result of the divine activity, or both, and it has these meanings in the Epistle to the Romans. With reference to the death of Christ, Paul wrote: "This was to show God's righteousness, because in his divine forbearance he had passed over former sins; it was to prove at the present time that he himself is righteous and that he justifies [reckons to be righteous] him who has faith in Jesus" (Rom. 3:25, 26).

We may summarize this section by stating that while God by his nature is perfectly righteous, in all his thoughts and actions, the meaning of righteousness in Scripture is primarily *that activity of God in the world in which he always does right.* Thus his righteousness has different effects and consequences in different situations.

But how do we distinguish between God as holy and as righteous since the two ideas appear to overlap or become equivalents? We are called in one place to be holy as God is holy (1 Pet. 1:16) while in another we are called to be righteous (Matt. 5:20). Holiness is the nature of God. Because he is light he cannot entertain any impurity and so he requires that his people also drive impurity from their lives. Purity must be their goal. Righteousness describes the nature, not of God in himself, but of God in his activity and relationships. All that he does is right. So he blesses one and punishes another, accepts one and rejects another. The effect of his righteousness is to create righteousness in men and women. Thus, as far as we are concerned, what God wants to achieve in us may be called either holiness or righteousness.

GOD IS ALWAYS FAITHFUL

The character of God cannot, of course, be separated from his own inner life expressed in the name of Yahweh. We have discussed the meaning of this name but have not yet quoted an interpretation of it supplied by God himself: "The Lord, the Lord, a God merciful and gracious, slow to anger, and abounding in steadfast love and faithfulness, keeping steadfast love for thousands, forgiving iniquity and transgression and sin, but who will by no means

clear the guilty, visiting the iniquity of the
fathers upon the children and the children's
children, to the third and the fourth generation"
(Exod. 34:6-8). From these words, and others like
them, we deduce that what God was in his
attitude to man in the moment in which he
spoke these sentences, he is now and will be
tomorrow, for he does not change in his
faithfulness. So we speak of his faithfulness
toward mankind and especially to his covenant
people. Indeed, it could be claimed that one of
the major themes of the Bible is the faithfulness
of God in keeping the covenant, be it the
covenant with Noah (Gen. 9:9-17), with
Abraham (Gen. 17:2, ff.), with Moses (Deut. 4),
or through Christ (Heb. 8:6).

The psalmist delighted to sing of the
faithfulness of God and of his entire trust-
worthiness:

> Thy steadfast love, O Lord, extends to the
> heavens,
> thy faithfulness to the clouds (Psa. 36:5).

> I have not hid thy saving help within my
> heart,
> I have spoken of thy faithfulness and thy
> salvation;
> I have not concealed thy steadfast love and
> thy faithfulness
> from the great congregation (Psa. 40:10).

> I will sing of thy steadfast love, O Lord,
> for ever;

with my mouth I will proclaim thy faithfulness to all generations.
For thy steadfast love was established for ever,
thy faithfulness is firm as the heavens
(Psa. 89:1, 2).

Is is good to give thanks to the Lord,
to sing praises to thy name, O Most High;
to declare thy steadfast love in the morning,
and thy faithfulness by night (Psa. 92:1, 2).

The words of Jeremiah are familiar to many:
"The steadfast love of the Lord never ceases,
his mercies never come to an end; they are new
every morning; great is thy faithfulness" (Lam.
3:22, 23).

In the New Testament the writers also
celebrate the faithfulness of God. "God is
faithful," declared Paul, "by whom you were
called into the fellowship of his Son, Jesus Christ
our Lord" (1 Cor. 1:9). The faithfulness of the
One who calls is the same as the One who
preserves: "No temptation has overtaken you
that is not common to man. God is faithful, and
he will not let you be tempted beyond your
strength, but with the temptation will also
provide the way of escape, that you may be able
to endure it" (1 Cor. 10:13, 14). And "He who
calls you is faithful, and he will do it"
(1 Thess. 5:24).

It is because God is faithful that Paul can
introduce into his pastoral Epistles what are
often called "the faithful sayings." The first of
these reads: "The saying is sure and worthy of

full acceptance, that Christ Jesus came into the world to save sinners" (1 Tim. 1:15; see also 4:8, 9; 2 Tim. 2:11-13; Tit. 3:4-8). Jesus Christ is portrayed elsewhere as the faithful High Priest, faithful in his work for God and faithful in his work for men (Heb. 2:17; 3:1), and a faithful witness both for God and man (Rev. 1:5; 3:7; 21:5; 22:6). God the Father is the faithful Father (Heb. 10:23; 11:11), faithful Creator (1 Pet. 4:19), and faithful forgiver of sins (1 John 1:9). The Holy Spirit is the faithful giver of divine life and sanctifier of God's people (2 Tim. 1:14).

It is sometimes asked, how can we reconcile the doctrine of the unchanging faithfulness of God to the idea that God changes his mind or is sorry for actions he took? First, let us note examples of the teaching that God does not change. "God is not man, that he should lie, or a son of man, that he should repent" (Num. 23:19). "The Glory of Israel will not lie or repent; for he is not a man, that he should repent" (1 Sam. 15:29). "Every good endowment and every perfect gift is from above, coming from the Father of lights with whom there is no variation or shadow due to change" (James 1:17). (Other passages of this kind are Psa. 110:4; Jer. 4:28; Ezek. 24:14; Zech. 8:14, and Mal. 3:6.)

Second, we note that with equal clarity there is teaching that God changes. "The Lord repented of the evil which he thought to do to his people" (Exod. 32:14). "Nevertheless he regarded their distress, when he heard their cry. He remembered for their sake his covenant, and relented according to the abundance of his steadfast love" (Psa. 106:45). "When God saw what they did, how they turned from their evil way, God repented of the evil which he had said he would do to them; and he did not do it" (Jonah 3:10). (Other passages of this kind are found in Gen. 6:6, ff.; Exod. 32:14; Jdg. 2:18; 1 Sam. 15:10, 11, 35; 2 Sam. 24:16; 1 Chron. 21:15; Jer. 18:8, 10; 26:3, 13, 19; 42:10; Amos 7:3, 6; Joel 2:13; Jonah 4:2.)

To deal with this topic adequately would take a whole book. Here we can only make basic suggestions. What God is teaching us in these passages describing his immutability and unchangeableness is that in his relation to his people, the people of his covenant, he is entirely trustworthy. To his people God gives his gifts and promises (Rom. 9:4; 11:29) and he never changes his mind in his intention to do good to and for his people. God is certainly not totally detached from his people in an isolated transcendence, but he is unchanging in his generosity to them.

In the passages which deal with the repentance of God we find that God responds to man in an ethical setting. Man's conduct is taken into account by God in order to make clear the moral integrity of God and for God to deal with man as a responsible moral being. Further, the repentance of God is often also an expression of his compassion and love. To say that God takes man's repentance into account is not to say that the covenant relationship is merely a bargain-counter experience. God always acts toward his people in a far richer way than ever they deserve.

117

It is interesting to note that the long, practical experience of the Israelites of the repentance of God makes its way into the description of God supplied by the later prophets. Joel described God as "gracious and merciful, slow to anger, and abounding in steadfast love, *and repents of evil*" (Joel 2:13), while Jonah said to God: "For I knew that thou art a gracious God and merciful, slow to anger, and abounding in steadfast love, *and repentest of evil*" (Jonah 4:2). If these two statements are compared with the description of God in Exodus 34:6, which belongs to the early period of the history of Israel, then it will be seen that there is no reference there to repenting by God.

THE UNCHANGING GOD AND CHANGING MAN

We began this chapter with a brief review of the way we are changing during our lifetime. We then looked at four ways in which God does not change. The problem we now face is to try to unravel how the fact of God's unchangeableness is significant for, and is to be given expression in, our lives.

In chapters four and five we looked at some of the problems that we face in any attempt to cope with the gulf between the temporal (in which we live) and the eternal (in which God lives). God is unchanging, while men change not only from year to year but from generation to generation. We live in a specific cultural heritage which runs as a stream through the present into the future.

In this book we have assumed a firm allegiance to the ancient creeds. This does not imply that our ideas of God have been frozen for 1,500 years. Rather, the creeds protect our understanding of God from falling into heresy, and the recital of the creeds can help to unite Christians of different denominations. To some the creeds may appear to be archaic. And the God to whom they point, therefore, may appear to be archaic. The unchanging God may seem to be entombed in an unchanged language and marooned or cut off from the onward drift of human culture and language.

As man changes, what God means to man changes; but the fact of God does not change. In each generation God is working to make the new creation which will replace this present one. It is therefore essential that we allow God to express himself and his will within our lives in our respective situations. We are not to conform to the standards of our culture but are to live within it as God's new creation so that he can work through us. What we do and say and how we do it and speak is to be determined by our allegiance to Jesus Christ, who is "the same yesterday and today and forever" (Heb. 13:8). We are not to escape from the real world in which we live and create for ourselves a kind of subculture in which only those in the circle understand our language and activities. Within the mainstream of human society and culture we are to be ambassadors of the unchanging Lord.

Human uncertainty is not eliminated when a person becomes a Christian. He is still subject to fear and depression; he has moments of insecurity and anxiety. Living in what we would call primitive conditions, the people of Israel also knew what uncertainty and fear were; and it was in such states of mind that they found great comfort in the unchanging faithfulness of God. Using imagery drawn from the countryside and culture they knew, they spoke of God as a rock, a fortress, a shield, and a refuge.

> The Lord is my rock, and my fortress, and
>   my deliverer,
> my God, my rock, in whom I take refuge,
> my shield, and the horn of my salvation, my
>   stronghold (Psa. 18:2).

> Yea, thou art my rock and my fortress;
> for thy name's sake lead me and guide me,
> take me out of the net which is hidden for me,
> for thou art my refuge.
> Into thy hands I commit my spirit;
> thou hast redeemed me, O Lord, faithful God
>   (Psa. 31:3-5).

> God is our refuge and strength,
> a very present help in trouble.
> Therefore we will not fear though the earth
>   should change,
> though the mountains shake in the heart of
>   the sea;

though its waters roar and foam,
though the mountains tremble with its
   tumult (Psa. 46:1-3).

Today in our own uncertainties, which are
seemingly increased by education, affluence, and
technological progress, we need to learn to see
God as the personal, unchangeable reality to
whom we can cling in the storms of doubts and
depression.

SEVEN
God Is Loving

Love is a word which carries a variety of meanings in modern English. An average person claims to love a special type of food, a specific place, a form of transport, a particular type of book, or a family pet. At the same time he or she claims to love other human beings and, if married, to make love to the partner. So we find ourselves using the word "love" to cover all kinds of human affections and desires. We also claim to "love" God and the Lord Jesus:

> My Jesus I love thee, I know thou art mine,
> For thee all the pleasures of sin I resign.

> King of glory, King of peace,
> I will love thee.

But often, soon after we have stated our love for God, we find ourselves expressing our love for mere manufactured objects—a new coat, a new car, or a box of chocolates.

In the Greek language, in which the New Testament is written and into which the Old Testament was translated from the Hebrew, there were three important words for "love." *Eros* was the irresistible sexual drive, the passionate yearning after another person. Our word "erotic" comes from this word. *Philia* was the liking of or caring for a friend or relative. It was also used to express love of a Greek or Roman god for a man or woman. *Agape* was the act of generosity to another, especially to one in need.

In the Bible *eros* is never used to describe the love of God for man, the love of man for God, or Christian love in the fellowship of the church. *Philia* is used of Christian love within the church, but *agape* is the word specifically used in the New Testament for the love of God toward man, for the love of God by men, and for Christian love to other human beings, especially enemies. So it is that the Christian community meal (1 Cor. 11) is called the *Agape* (the love-feast), and as such, it was practiced by the early Methodists and has been revived in recent times by several different types of churches.

The availability of these different words meant that the apostles and the first Christians were able to be much more specific when they spoke of God's love than we are. The confusion within our own language puts a greater demand upon us to be very careful when we speak publicly of what we mean by *agape*.

For John, the basic reason for loving others is that "love [*agape*] is of God" and "God is love" (1 John 4:7, 8). For Paul, the One whom he serves and preaches is "the God of love" (2 Cor. 13:11).

In the Gospel of John, the love of the Father for the Son and of the Son for the Father is frequently mentioned. The Father loved the Son before the foundation of the world (John 17:24) and loves him still because he laid down his life for the sins of the human race (John 10:17). The Son loves the Father by carrying out the task given to him by the Father (John 14:31; 15:10). The Holy Spirit communicates the love of God to human beings (John 16:14). To John's teaching Paul adds that "God's love has been poured into our hearts through the Holy Spirit which has been given to us" (Rom. 5:5).

The Father loves the Son eternally in the Holy Spirit, and the Son loves the Father eternally in the Holy Spirit. God is a Trinity of Love. To explain this to people theologians have used the analogy of the lover (the Father), the loved one (the Son), and the bond of love between them (the Holy Spirit). Like all analogies this helps some people and not others. The great problem with all attempts to illustrate the doctrine of the Holy Trinity is that they seek to achieve the impossible. The Trinity of Love is unique and is ultimately a mystery into which we cannot probe.

But what do we mean when we say that God in himself is love? If a human being has too high an estimation of himself we tend to think that he is self-centered and lacking in concern for others. We feel that a true Christian will love others as much as he loves himself. So it is asked, "If God is love, how can God love himself so fully?" The answer probably goes something like this: Love by its very nature must desire, work for, and create that which is excellent. We know from experience that truly to love another is to want the best for that person. God, being infinite and eternal, is perfect and excellent in himself; therefore, he can do no other than love himself. In holy love God perfectly loves himself.

Yet, since God is *agape* and it is of the nature of *agape* to be generous to others, especially the needy, God also loves that which lies outside himself—his creation. So we claim that God's activity of creating and redeeming us is a demonstration of his eternal and holy love. God himself, being perfect love, loves perfectly.

GOD'S LOVE FOR ISRAEL IN THE OLD TESTAMENT

The creation of the world was seen as both the result of God's "steadfast love" and as giving pleasure to the God of love (Gen. 1:4, 10, 31). In Psalm 136 the recital of the creation of various parts of the universe is linked with the chorus, "for his steadfast love endures forever." After Adam and Eve's disobedience God did not relegate mankind to its own pernicious devices, but he promised to redeem it (Gen. 3:15). When Noah's generation had no time for the Lord he still showed favor and grace to Noah's family and made a new covenant of grace and blessing with the human race (Gen. 9:1-17). Abraham, Isaac, and Jacob were taken under the special protection and guidance of Yahweh and so their descendants could be described as God's "first-born son" (Exod. 4:22).

The covenant which God made with the people of Israel at Sinai (Exod. 19:4, ff.; 34:9, ff.; Deut. 4:31; 7:7, ff.) was a demonstration of Yahweh's mercy and kindness. This is a theme we noted in studying the faithfulness of God (Exod. 34:6, ff.) and which comes also in the Psalms:

> But thou, O Lord, art a God merciful and
> gracious,
> slow to anger and abounding in steadfast love
> and faithfulness (Psa. 86:15).

> The Lord is merciful and gracious,
> slow to anger and abounding in steadfast
> love (Psa. 103:8).

This mercy and love, being God's love, is holy love and as such cannot be rejected or spurned without dire consequences.

The Lord is "a jealous God" (Exod. 20:5; Deut. 5:9). How can jealousy be a part of love? Again we are back to the problem of anthropomorphic language. Holy love is perfect and offers the very best. Holy love is not sentimental or sloppy. For the Israelites to turn from the living, holy Lord and to worship idols was a serious rejection of both the mercy which brought them into the covenant and the steadfast love which supported them within the covenant. Holy love cannot tolerate human worship and affection being offered to idols. Holy love cannot tolerate the actions of those who are being loved when they turn from God to pursuits which end in their own destruction. God is jealous of his own name and he is not prepared to allow his holy love to be spurned by his people.

To illustrate God's love for Israel a variety of images are used. God is the caring shepherd: "I will surely gather all of you, O Jacob, I will gather the remnant of Israel; I will set them together like sheep in a fold, like a flock in its pasture" (Mic. 2:12). He is the concerned physician: "Return, O faithless sons, I will heal your faithlessness" (Jer. 3:22). He is the gracious Savior: "I, I am the Lord, and besides me there is no Savior" (Isa. 43:11). He is the faithful Bridegroom: "I plighted my troth to you and entered into a covenant with you, says the Lord God, and you became mine" (Ezek. 16:8). Above all, he is the Father of his people so that they are his first-born son (Exod. 4:22). He is the Father of kings (2 Sam. 7:13, ff.; Psa. 89:26, ff.), of orphans (Psa. 68:5), and of those who reverence him (Psa. 103:13). Sometimes the love of Yahweh is said to be greater than that of a mother for her child; for example, God, through Isaiah said,

But Zion said, "The Lord has forsaken me, my Lord has forgotten me."
"Can a woman forget her sucking child,

that she should have no compassion on the
son of her womb?"
Even these may forget,
yet will I not forget you (Isa. 49:14, 15).

and

As one whom his mother comforts,
so I will comfort you;
you shall be comforted in Jerusalem
(Isa. 66:13).

In words spoken by Jeremiah the Lord told Israel:
"I have loved you with an everlasting love;
therefore I have continued my faithfulness to
you" (Jer. 31:3). The fact of the love of God to
Israel means that when Israel has sinned, God is
always waiting to restore and forgive her (Jer.
3:12, 14, 22; 4:1; Ezek. 16:53-63; Isa. 49:15;
54:5-8; 62:4, ff.).

Perhaps the most vivid and memorable
portrayal of God's love for Israel is provided in
the book of Hosea, the prophet. When Hosea
describes God as if he were a man wooing, loving,
and marrying an unworthy woman who is a
prostitute, and doing this against all convention,
law, and reason, he is declaring that God's love
and relationship with his people is deeper than
any legal form can allow. There are many
moving extracts that could be quoted. Here is
but one:

How can I give you up, O Ephraim!
How can I hand you over, O Israel!

    ... My heart recoils within me,
  my compassion grows warm and tender
    (Hos. 11:8).

God continued to love an unworthy people
when what they deserved was severe punishment for their unfaithfulness to the covenant.

    Though God's love as described in the Old
Testament is primarily a protecting and caring
love for Israel, there are hints that God's love
is also for the whole world (see Deut. 33:3; Isa.
42:6; Mal. 2:10). This theme is more fully
developed in the New Testament.

GOD'S LOVE FOR THE WORLD
IN THE NEW TESTAMENT

As in the Old Testament, so in the New, the
image of God as Father is an important means
for conveying the truth that God is *agape*. God's
love is a Father's love. Jesus called his disciples to
love their enemies since the Father in heaven
sends the rain and the sunshine on both evil and
good people (Matt. 5:45). To this same Father
their prayers were to be addressed (Matt. 6:9-12).
   We must remember when reading of our
Father in heaven that this imagery was used
within a Jewish culture. In such a situation the
loving rule of the father in the household and
the stability of the family were taken for granted.
Today, in our Western society with the
"nuclear" family and the one-parent home, the
image of the loving but firm father is not so
prominent. This means that when we read the

Bible we must not read into it our ideas of what a particular father may be like today; rather, we must think of the highest ideal of the first-century Jewish father and remind ourselves that this is the image which helps us to know what God, the Father, is like.

Because God is the Creator and Sustainer of everything, there is a real sense in which he is the loving Father of all humanity and so he is portrayed as loving the whole human race. Paul speaks of God our Savior "who desires all men to be saved and come to the knowledge of the truth" (1 Tim. 2:3, ff.; 4:10). In a memorable verse John speaks of God who so loved the world that he gave his only Son (John 3:16). However, he is the Father in a special sense of those who believe in Jesus Christ. The eternal Father loves the eternal Son (John 15:9); therefore he has a special love for those who by faith and the Holy Spirit are united to the Son (Rom. 8:28-30). Thus Christians are called the adopted sons of God (Gal. 4:4-7). And as children who are loved, they are sometimes chastised in order that they might learn to be true children (Heb. 12:6).

The direction of the love of God is always toward sinners; this includes those who have not yet responded to the gospel and those who, having responded, are sinners being made holy. This means that the love of God provides sinners with forgiveness (Matt. 6:12, 14, 15; 18:21, ff.). It also makes those who have been his enemies into his adopted, obedient children.

Paul is very clear in his understanding of the new situation introduced into the world by

God's love in Jesus Christ. The conclusion to the weighty contents of Romans 1—8 is a summary of what he has been demonstrating; that is, "the love of God in Christ Jesus our Lord" (Rom. 8:28-39). This tremendous assurance of divine love rests on three facts. First, God the Father sent the Son into the world; this great act of love was perfected on the cross in the self-offering of the incarnate Son (Rom. 5:6-11). Second, God loves men by calling them, according to his eternal plans, into the Kingdom of his Son and into the fellowship of his Body, the Church (Rom. 5:10, 11). Third, God's love is poured into the hearts of those who believe the gospel (Rom. 5:5; 8:9, ff.).

Even as Jesus did not distinguish between his own activity and that of God but rather did what God alone could do in granting the forgiveness of sins, so for Paul, the love of God is basically the same as the love of Christ (Rom. 8:39). God's loving activity is revealed and realized in the loving work of Christ: "But God shows his love for us in that while we were yet sinners Christ died for us" (Rom. 5:8). The eternal love of God becomes in the love of Christ a world-changing event. It creates new people for God, a people who are constrained and controlled by divine love (2 Cor. 5:14), whose lives portray the fruit of the Spirit, which is love (Gal. 5:22). Thus it is stated that "Christ loved the Church and gave himself up for her" (Eph. 5:25).

The love of God provides the means whereby we can enter into fellowship with the holy Lord.

Fellowship with him means that his love is in our hearts and we can love him instead of, as previously, hating him. The same love, in the power of the Holy Spirit, enables us to love other human beings. Paul told the Galatians: "Through love be servants of one another. For the whole law is fulfilled in one word, 'You shall love your neighbor as yourself' " (Gal. 5:13, 14). Loving other human beings often leads them to seek to know God and thereby the circle of divine love is completed. God loves us: we love him and we love others; others begin to love God and their neighbors. In this sense it is love which makes the world go 'round. Each local church should be a community of loving. Each Christian home should be a home of love.

We may summarize the nature of the love of God for us and through us in the following points.

1. God's love is a universal love (John 3:16).

2. God's love is a love we do not deserve (Rom. 5:8).

3. God's love is a sacrificial love. The Father gave the Son for us (1 John 4:9, 10), and the Son loved us and gave himself for us (Gal. 2:20).

4. God's love outlasts all human love and is for eternity (Rom. 8:39).

5. God's love saves us from the guilt of sin and makes us holy (2 Thess. 2:13).

6. God's love strengthens us in our fight against evil (Rom. 8:37).

7. God's love disciplines us (Heb. 12:6).

8. God's love brings its own rewards (James 1:12; 2:5).

This *agape* which we receive should be in us, pass through us, and be felt by our families (Eph. 5:25, 28, 33), our Christian brothers and sisters (1 Pet. 2:17), our neighbors (James 2:8), and our enemies (Luke 6:27).

While the study of the love of God enriches our experience, elevates our minds, and warms our hearts, we cannot avoid questions about it which sometimes are asked by sincere Christians and seekers after truth.

Question: If God loves the world why do some people go to hell?   A simple way to answer this question is to deny that any people go finally to hell and to affirm that God's love is universal and will, therefore, ultimately insure that all people come to enjoy eternal life with God in heaven. Though this type of answer is attractive it is, in fact, only superficially attractive. If we take seriously the words of Jesus and his apostles, then we find that they certainly taught that those who stubbornly continue to reject the love of God will be judged and punished by God. Surely this is the force of several of the parables of Jesus (e.g., Matt. 25, where there are three parables) as well as the plain meaning of statements in the Epistles (e.g., 2 Thess. 1:6-10).

To say "no" to God's offer of salvation is to remain a recipient of the wrath and the judgment of God. In the gospel, God's love provides an answer to the eternal needs of humanity; a man cannot enter the way of salvation because he is a sinner, a fact which leaves him quite unable to help himself. Therefore, for him to reject the gospel is to remain in sin and in opposition to God. This means that he is under the divine judgment, for the holy God must punish sinners. If he did not he would not remain the holy God. In Christ, he has punished sinners; in Christ, an atonement for sin is provided and to reject this is to deserve God's judgment. So it is both biblical and rational to state that God condemns to punishment those who have made it clear that they do not want to enjoy his grace and eternal salvation.

But this does not answer the question; it merely clears the ground to answer the question. Our specific problem relates to those who have not heard the gospel because where they live there is neither church nor evangelist. Various solutions have been suggested to the problem. One states that the only way to God is by faith in Jesus Christ and, therefore, pagans who never hear the gospel cannot possibly go to heaven. To argue thus is probably to make deductions that the Bible does not make—for it does not address itself to this question. Another solution is to state that God will judge each man according to his own light—e.g., what kind of Buddhist or Muslim a man has been. A further solution is to state that God will judge according to moral law, that law which is written into our consciences and summarized in the Ten Commandments. The thinking behind this is that if we are not living in the covenant of grace, then we must be living in the covenant of works and judged by moral law.

In the end we have to admit that we do not

know what will be the fate of the sincere Hindu, Buddhist, or animist who has never heard the gospel. We refrain from being dogmatic and, as a positive act, we support the new churches and missionary work so that such people will soon be able to hear in their own languages the gospel of the grace of God.

Question: Why does God allow such terrible suffering?   The problem of suffering has always been with man and probably will always be with him. There is no easy solution to it. However, it is possible to provide certain lines of thought which may help some to accept suffering in such a way that faith in God and trust in his love are still possible and meaningful.

First of all, it must be noted that there would be no problem of evil or suffering if we did not believe in a good and loving God. If there is no God, or if there is a God who is not loving, there is every reason why evil and suffering should exist in the world. It is only when we believe in the existence of a good God and accept the reality of evil (unlike, for example, the Hindu who believes that evil is an illusion) that the problem of suffering actually arises.

It is helpful to differentiate between the different kinds of evil. There is what is called moral evil. This is evil which is caused by man to man. No one can deny that, as society has become more advanced technologically, so also have the means of human destruction become more sophisticated and refined. Men always seem to be ingenious in devising ways of torturing and of being cruel to their fellowmen. The invention of bombs which can do immense damage is but one example.

Yet to blame man for all the evil in the world is not satisfactory. Why, it may be asked, did God create man with the freedom to follow evil inclinations and to bring so much suffering into the world? Could God not have made man in such a way that, although he might desire to do evil, he would nevertheless be prevented from doing so? But this, we must admit, would have meant making automatons and not human beings who have genuine freedom to exercise their wills and choose good rather than evil. If God created man so that man might love him freely and spontaneously, then he could not have made him to do good only.

There is also what is called physical evil— earthquakes and famines for example. These are certainly not caused by man but are part of the physical universe in which he lives. We often ask ourselves: Can we absolve God from the responsibility of this kind of evil when it exists in a world which he has created? Perhaps it needs to be emphasized that the universe must work according to certain principles which provide a general predictable reliability in order to provide the kind of environment necessary for the moral development of free human beings. For example, gravitational attraction prevents the earth from flying apart or straying from its orbit around the sun. It also, of course, seals a man's destruction when he falls from a high place.

Traditional Christian teaching, based on the Bible, has been that with the entry of sin into the lives of human beings came also the entry of some disorder into the fabric of the created world. The result of this judgment of God was the subjection of the created order to certain laws of nature which can result in the destruction of human and animal life—hurricanes and earthquakes, for example. Also, after the entry of sin human existence became a toilsome burden (Gen. 3:14, ff.).

Physical evil has also been attributed to the devil and to demonic forces in the world. This may seem incredible to people who live in an advanced, technological society, but it can find some justification in the teaching of Genesis 2—3. It must be remembered, however, that there is no ultimate source of evil as a reality in addition to God. God is sovereign and nothing happens which he does not permit. In the new heaven and earth, which is to come, there will be no evil.

Yet whatever reason is offered for the existence of physical evil, Paul teaches that the whole of the creation groans as it awaits its own liberation at the revelation of the sons of God (Rom. 8:18-25). The bondage to which it is subjected will be broken at the end of the age when this new heaven and earth appear.

The arguments we have just advanced may help some people to accept the fact of evil and suffering as a necessary part of present human existence on earth. Yet they may still ask the question, "Why does suffering appear to come so haphazardly?" Both good people and bad people experience tragedy. This must remain a mystery. Only God knows each of us sufficiently to see why suffering is the lot of particular individuals.

Nevertheless, the situation is not irredeemable. It is because suffering falls so haphazardly that it brings forth the feelings of compassion and human sympathy for those who are unfortunate. Not that such feelings justify the existence of suffering, but the situation as it is makes them possible. If each time a person was struck down with an incurable disease or by lightning it was seen to be a just punishment for a sin that person had committed, then human suffering would soon become a matter of indifference. People's behavior would also be motivated by the results expected and by self-interest with self-preservation, rather than for the good of others.

It is sobering to remember that for those who have to suffer in this world there is nothing more aggravating than to be given pious platitudes and all-too-easy solutions or merely to be told, "it is the will of God." God does not desire that his creatures should suffer. However, he does use suffering to bring about his desired will for any individual because he chooses to work within the fallen world as it exists. (In chapter eight we shall look more closely at the subject of God's wrath and punishment of sin.)

In retrospect we often look back with wonder at the way in which certain apparently disastrous experiences turned out for our welfare. We declare that they could not have happened accidentally. In such reflection we are making use of our conviction that "in everything God works for good with those who love him" (Rom. 8:28). But we must distinguish between events as they are, or have been, and events as seen through the faith which later thought evokes or uses.

One of the intriguing aspects of suffering is that very often the experience of suffering is worse for those looking on than for those actually suffering. Sometimes there is a mysterious power at work in those who are suffering so that relatives and friends are baffled. This serves to remind us that evil and suffering pose a problem because we believe in a good God who is active in creation and in the lives of his people. God himself did not remain aloof from suffering but entered this world and, in Jesus Christ, endured suffering of mind and body on our behalf. So "we have not a High Priest who is unable to sympathize with our weaknesses, but one who in every respect has been tempted as we are, yet without sin" (Heb. 4:15).

Our attitude toward suffering determines how we respond to it, and one key to the most constructive attitude would seem to be humble acceptance. It is only when we have reached the point of acceptance and submission that we allow God's creative agency to begin a new work within our hearts and transform tragedy into triumph. The mental struggle may continue and moments of depression may occur, but those

who are submitted to the loving, righteous
Lord will have found in him an anchor for their
souls, an anchor which is steadfast and sure
and which enables them to endure the storms
of life and to come out of them rejoicing in the
love and faithfulness of God.

IS ALL LOVE OF GOD?

To assert that God is love is not to be
sentimental. To identify God as love requires, as
we have shown, a particular understanding of
love as *agape*. It is foolish to claim that just
any kind of love manifests God's love, for we
know from experience that anything from
adultery to euthanasia can be *called* love. How
then is the Christian to recognize God's love
in the turmoil of modern life?

Some Christians try to make easy the
recognition of God's love by isolating it as
something specific in personal experience. Yet
we mistake the nature of God's love to suppose
that as human beings we can ever totally isolate
it. Some people suggest that God's love is merely
a Christian interpretation of the Christian
experience of, and in, the world. Yet one of the
themes which has emerged in our study of God's
nature is *his initiative in interpreting himself
to mankind*.

God's love draws man to himself. God's love
is an ongoing activity, attitude, and approach.
By the Holy Spirit God reveals his love to, in,
and through human beings in a variety of ways.
Man on his own initiative cannot reveal the love

of God. God's love is nothing less than his total saving activity toward, in, and through us. If we attempt to specify what God's love means to us or to our church fellowship, all we offer is a glimpse of the greater totality of love.

Human beings easily fall prey to sentimental nostalgia. Wonderful blessings from yesterday are recalled with fondness and heard with eagerness. God's love known in the past is recited in the present as a reminder that God loves now. God's love is a reality which is concerned with real people in vital situations. God's love reaches into the palace as much as into the gutter; it reaches beyond the barriers of luxury and poverty, of ambition and idleness, of tolerance and intolerance, of knowledge and ignorance, and of fear and courage. It is in his love to us that God is known to be Love. God's love was proclaimed and exhibited once for all in the life and death of Jesus Christ. In the present, the same love of God through Christ in the power of the loving Spirit is active in bringing men to the Father. It is not just a question of God so loving the world a long time ago. Rather it is a question of God loving in the past and loving just as much now.

We love God, love our fellow Christians, and love our enemies only because God has first loved us and loves us still. All true *agape* can be traced to God. Further, God's love shows the extent of God's claim upon us. In his love God is demanding toward us. Therefore, we now turn to look at this further aspect of our knowledge of God.

EIGHT
God Is Demanding

At one time or another most human beings feel that they ought to exert themselves in order to help others. For example, if a person is walking down the street behind someone who stumbles and falls, he feels he ought to help him to his feet. Various explanations of such helpful behavior are possible and are offered by both psychologists and sociologists; but for the Christian, the best answer will be in terms of the voice of conscience. This voice is a part of what it means to be made in the image and likeness of God (Gen. 1:27; Rom. 2:5-11).

The conscience of the Christian should in fact be sharper than that of other people, for within his conscience (heart) God has written both his gospel and his law (see the nature of the new covenant as outlined in Jer. 31:31, ff.). This is the new law of Christ, the implications of which are given in the Sermon on the Mount and in the command to love one another.

But why, it is asked, does God require such high standards of thought, attitude, and behavior from us? Why are we called to live the perfect life of loving God and man? Ultimately, the answer to these important questions is that God is perfect, righteous, and holy and that he calls his creatures, and particularly his adopted children, to be perfect as he is perfect (Matt. 5:48).

DEPENDENCE INCLUDES APPROPRIATE RESPONSE

As we noted in chapter three, our relationship to God, whether we are conscious of it or not, is always one of creaturely dependence. As creatures we are required by our Creator, who is perfectly just, to live in such a manner as pleases him and is appropriate to our role as creatures. Usually we explain this response in terms of obeying the Ten Commandments, keeping the moral law, or loving God and our neighbors.

The entry of sin into the world through the disobedience of Adam and Eve did not cause the demands of God either to increase or decrease. From the pre-Fall as well as the sinful Adam, God required the perfect response of trust and obedience. And, since Adam, throughout the history of mankind up to the present day, God has not ceased to make a total demand upon all his creatures.

Human sin is offensive to God and, because of who he is and his nature, God has finally to deal with sin. This means punishing those who commit it. All the human race is in the position of offending God by being sinners and by failing to give him the trust and obedience which he, as Creator, Sustainer, and Ruler, requires.

One of the glorious themes of the Bible is that God's love provided for the human race what his justice and righteousness demanded of human beings. This provision, begun in the period immediately following Adam's sin, reached its climax and fulfillment in the incarnation of the Son of God, who, as our representative and Savior, lived, died, rose from the dead, and ascended into heaven for us. In Christ, God was reconciling the world to himself so that Jesus Christ is now the way, the truth, and the life (2 Cor. 5:17-21; John 14:6).

Therefore, though God still demands perfect trust and obedience from his creatures, he now accepts that which Christ did on our behalf instead of our own attempts to save ourselves. The only condition he makes is that we are united to Christ in faith and love. The result of such saving faith is that we know that God's demands upon us have been satisfied by the Lord Jesus and therefore we are free to love God sincerely. As we do this we know that our love of him will not be the means of earning his favor, but a means of pleasing him.

I would not work my soul to save,
for that my Lord has done;
But I would work like any slave,
for love of God's dear Son.

God's demands in terms of giving us eternal life have been satisfied for us by our Savior; but, God's demands upon us which arise from his holy and righteous love are constant: this is why we are called to love him with heart, soul, mind and strength, and to love our neighbors as we love ourselves. We have been delivered from the wrath to come in order that we might serve God now with joyful and willing lives.

To those who are not united to Jesus Christ in faith and love, God continues to be the demanding Creator who expects from them worship, trust, and obedience. When that worship due to him is offered to someone or something else (e.g., to an idol or to a material comfort), or when his demands of morality are not heeded, then the demanding God becomes the angry God. His wrath "is revealed from heaven against all ungodliness and wickedness of men" (Rom. 1:18).

We are much happier discussing the love of God than the wrath of God. But to present a full, biblical perspective of God, we must now show that the God who is always demanding is also sometimes the God who is angry.

GOD'S WRATH AS PORTRAYED
IN THE OLD TESTAMENT

In chapter one, in showing that God is personal and has to be described in anthropomorphic terms, we referred briefly to the description of God as snorting in anger. In fact, there are many references in the Old Testament to the anger of

God, often described in powerful imagery.

Some images are: an inner fire whose effect is that of making God to snort, foam, boil and release pent-up energy (Isa. 30:27, ff.; 34:5-10); a flame and a storm (Psa. 2:11; Isa. 13:13; Jer. 15:14; 30:23; Psa. 83:15). God's anger is seen in his reaction to the breaking of the covenant by the Israelites (Num. 11:1; 17:6-13; 13:25—14:38; Deut. 1:34, ff.) as it is also seen in his judgment when they turned to worship idols (Exod. 32; Num. 25; Deut. 11:16, ff.; 12:29—13:18; 29:15-20). The prophets declared that the anger of God was evoked through the despising of the divine love by Israel (Hos. 5:10; 8:5; Isa. 9:11; Jer. 4:4; Ezek. 5:13; 7:3).

Historical disasters—droughts, famines, epidemics, and plagues—were attributed to the divine wrath (Num. 11:1, 10; 12:9; 2 Sam. 24). The greatest example of God's wrath was the sending of the people from Palestine into Babylon in 586 B.C. (Jer. 27). Yet, when Israel repents and seeks God, then his wrath is turned away—for where there is no longer any deliberate sin and wickedness there is no longer need for divine wrath (Isa. 51:17, 22; 40:2; Jer. 4:4; 36:7).

Sometimes God's wrath was directed against specific individuals within Israel. Illness, affliction or premature death are seen in these cases as the result of divine wrath. The psalmist wrote:

Thy wrath has swept me over;
thy dread assaults destroy me.

> They surround me like a flood all day long;
> they close in upon me together (Psa. 88:16, 17).

Similar passages occur in Psalms 90:7, ff. and 102:9-12.

The wrath of God was also directed against nations around Israel. Through Ezekiel, God passed his sentence upon the Philistines: "I will execute great vengeance upon them with wrathful chastisements. Then they will know that I am the Lord, when I lay my vengeance upon them" (Ezek. 25:17). God was angry with the Philistines because of the way they treated his covenant people. Through Isaiah God actually described the Assyrians as the rod of his anger (Isa. 10:5) when he used them to chastise his people, Israel.

God's wrath may be defined as his offended love, justice, and righteousness. God is always loving, just and righteous. He is angry only when his love is spurned, his justice abandoned, and his righteousness mocked.

GOD'S WRATH AS PORTRAYED IN THE NEW TESTAMENT

Jesus did not hesitate, when the situation demanded it, to teach both by word and action that the wrath of God is a reality. In some of his parables he taught that God is angry with sinners. In the parable of the marriage feast (Matt. 22) God's judgment falls upon those who attend the feast improperly dressed and the meaning is that God's gifts of grace cannot be flouted by man. The actions of Jesus were sometimes deliberate, undisguised expressions of the divine anger. When the religious leaders watched Jesus to see whether he would heal on the Sabbath in order that they might accuse him, we read that Jesus "looked around at them with anger, grieved at their hardness of heart" (Mark 3:5). On another occasion when he saw how the holy Temple of Jerusalem was being misused by the priests and others he became angry and cleansed the Temple (John 2:14, ff.).

One of his sternest sayings was against those who deliberately put stumbling blocks in the way of the immature: "Whoever causes one of these little ones who believe in me to sin, it would be better for him to have a great millstone fastened round his neck and to be drowned in the depth of the sea" (Matt. 18:6). Jesus also revealed the divine anger against all forms of hypocrisy. The "woes" of Matthew 23 make very sober reading and stand always as a prophetic word against mere outward religion.

Not only did Jesus reveal the wrath of God against sin but he also took the full impact of it in himself. What we deserved he bore. He fulfilled what was written of the Suffering Servant of God in Isaiah 53. The cup to which he referred when he prayed in agony in the Garden of Gethsemane (Matt. 26:39; John 12:27) was the cup of God's wrath (cf., Isa. 51:17). Paul interpreted this by teaching that "Christ redeemed us from the curse of the law, having become a curse for us" (Gal. 3:13), and that Christ who knew no sin, God made to be sin on our behalf (2 Cor. 5:21). The incarnate Son of God, though sinless, experienced the wrath of God toward sinners. Not that God was angry with himself, but that God was angry with the sins of mankind, the just penalty of which Jesus Christ bore for us, so that we need not bear it ourselves.

The most studied passage in the New Testament in the effort to understand the nature of the wrath of God is Romans 1:18, ff. Here Paul insists that the non-Jewish world cannot offer the excuse that it has no knowledge of God because it has not been favored with the special revelation granted to Israel. God has revealed himself through his creation so that his everlasting power and divinity can be known. The proper deduction from this knowledge is that God should be worshiped. But, through sin, the population of the world has failed in this obligation and the demands of God have not been met. Instead of worshiping the supreme, living Lord, people have worshiped man-made idols. Therefore, the wrath of God is revealed from heaven against such perversion. Only when men turn from idolatry and immorality to serve the living God through Jesus Christ are they no longer under the wrath of God.

The simple proof that God is angry with sinners is seen in the universal fact of death (Gen. 3; Rom. 5:11, ff.). Even those who are joined to Christ have to pass through death. However, for them is the certainty of the resurrection of the dead, a benefit won for them by Christ. But for those who die in a state of rebellion against God, the only future they have is one of further experience of the results of the wrath of God (Matt. 25:30).

If we could rightly interpret human history we would, no doubt, find examples of God's wrath in the present age in terms of disasters and tragedies. Yet the full measure of his wrath will not be seen or experienced until the final day of judgment. The prophets of the old covenant spoke of the day of the Lord when Yahweh would vindicate the righteousness of his people against their enemies (Mal. 4:1). The writers of the New Testament look forward to the Second Coming of Christ as the time when there will be a universal judgment. Paul spoke of "the day of wrath when God's righteous judgment will be revealed" (Rom. 2:5), and of "the punishment of eternal destruction and exclusion from the presence of the Lord and from the glory of his might" (2 Thess. 1:9).

Therefore, as in the Old Testament, we see that the wrath of God is the reaction of holy love and righteousness to the rejection and misuse of the gifts and grace of God by mankind.

DEATH—A CONSTANT
REMINDER OF THE DEMANDING GOD

All of us at sometime or another come face to face with death. Though the death of thousands as shown on our TV screen usually makes little impression upon us, death in more immediate contexts deeply shocks us. To witness death in an automobile accident, to watch a loved one slowly die of cancer, and to see the victim of a cruel murder, these are experiences which deeply affect our emotions.

Yet, it is hard for us to grasp, as we confront death, that it occurs because God is demanding and we are sinners. To the person who is familiar with the themes of Scripture, the reality of death is a constant reminder that God and sin are totally opposed and can never be joined.

Death as a universal reality is part of God's judgment upon sin. It entered the human race after Adam and Eve disobeyed God and it will remain as a major factor in human experience until the end of this age at the final judgment of all peoples and the resurrection of the dead. For those who have sinned and remain unforgiven by God through Christ, death is the first part of the divine condemnation. The second part is eternal separation from God. As we have already noted, for those who become obedient to God by accepting the gospel and thus have their sins forgiven, death remains; but, for Christ's sake, this divine condemnation is reversed at the resurrection when Christians are given new bodies (1 Cor. 15).

God, as the righteous One, makes demands upon his creatures. Whether the persons be Adam and Eve, Abraham and Sarah, Moses and Joshua, Peter and Paul, or Queen Victoria and Prince Albert, God always demands faith in himself and obedience to his will. When men and women reject God and place their confidence in material things or creatures, then God in his holy justice is offended; his wrath is kindled. The universal sinfulness of mankind means that there is universal death—for this is one aspect of the wrath of God. The experience of death ought to remind us that mankind has failed to meet the demands of God and that there is laid upon each of us an obligation to seek with all our might to satisfy the demands which he still places upon us as his redeemed creatures.

DEMANDS AND COMMANDS

We began this chapter by referring to the voice of conscience which is part of every human being. The demanding God intends that our consciences should be instructed more and more concerning his will so that they become more alert and more tender. God's demands are often known by us in terms of commands. Let us illustrate this with particular reference to the individual Christian life.

Both Jesus and his apostles had quite a lot to teach about the control of the mind, its thoughts and imaginations. In the Sermon on the Mount, Jesus clearly showed that God's demands do not stop at our skins, with outward behavior. They penetrate into our hearts, minds, and consciences. All the Jews knew the commandment, "Thou shalt not commit adultery," but Jesus explained that this covered the desire and intention as well as the act itself (Matt. 5:27, ff.). Paul taught his converts to bring every thought into captivity to Christ so that Christ ruled every thought. Also, he advised that we should think about whatever is true, honorable, just, pure, lovely, gracious, and excellent (Phil. 4:8).

Why did Jesus and Paul call for full control over our inner lives? Because God is both all-knowing and righteous. Therefore, since he knows our inner life, his righteousness and justice require that both in thought and deed we conform to his will (1 Thess. 4:3, 4).

Jesus and his apostles also had much to say about the nature of the worship which we offer to God. Because God is Spirit—that is, holy, righteous Spirit—he is to be worshiped spiritually and according to truth (John 4:24). The nature of God as self-existent Spirit demands that he be worshiped in a manner appropriate to his being. This means that we are to worship him with our whole heart and according to the revelation he has given us. Thus the demands that God makes upon his churches in terms of public worship must be taken very seriously.

The character of God as faithful and just demands that we regularly repent of our sins in order to be cleansed: "If we say we have no sin, we deceive ourselves, and the truth is not in us. If we confess our sins, he is faithful and just, and will forgive our sins and cleanse us from all unrighteousness" (1 John 1:8, 9). The character of God as love also means that we are to love him and others: "Beloved, let us love one another; for love is of God, and he who loves is born of God and knows God. He who does not love does not know God, for God is love" (1 John 4:7, 8).

God is demanding. He demands and commands that we obey his will. As Christians, our joy and duty is to seek the help of the Holy Spirit in order that we may delight to satisfy his demands of love and righteousness.

NINE
God Is Dependable

We feel our weaknesses and inadequacies at different times and levels in our lives. Perhaps we have a friend who is an alcoholic and we feel helpless to assist him; perhaps we are overwhelmed by certain intellectual questions (e.g., the problem of suffering) and we feel incapable of answering them; perhaps our knees begin to knock at the prospect of taking part in the visitation of houses on behalf of Christ and the local church. Then, at the local church level, especially when we examine our corporate life and activity we often feel that our performance has been totally inadequate in terms of worship, outreach to the neighborhood, and caring for the needy.

We are told that our inadequacies should cause us to trust God more. This is right. In practice, it means that we trust him directly as our heavenly Father and as he ministers to us through our sisters and brothers in the Body of Christ. Since our concern here is with the doctrine of God, we must now attempt to answer the question: What do we mean when we claim in choruses that "Christ is the answer to my every need," and "My God shall supply your every need . . ."? Or, in plain terms, what have we in mind when we say that God is adequate?

GOD HAS NO NEEDS
HIMSELF AND HE SUPPLIES OUR NEEDS

God is adequate in himself. He does not need any assistance from his creation. His own life and existence are not dependent upon angels, archangels, cherubim, or human beings. He is complete in himself. We developed this theme when we discussed the fact that God is unchanging in himself and toward his people. It is, of course, the fact that God is adequate in himself that enables him to supply our every need. He is to us the adequate Lord.

As we should expect, the adequacy of God is a theme which is not ignored in the Old Testament. Not only is it taught in the direct oracles of God through the psalmists and prophets, it is a deduction we can rightfully make from the experience of individuals who had a vital relationship with God. Take, for example, the life of Abraham, and especially his readiness to offer to God his only son, the son of promise, through whose life and descendants all the promises of God were to be fulfilled (Gen. 22:1-10). According to the Epistle to the Hebrews, so great was the confidence of Abraham in the adequacy of God that he believed God would raise Isaac from the dead (Heb. 11:19).

Direct statements about the adequacy of God are many. First of all we may quote from Psalm 56. The psalmist confessed:

> When I am afraid,
> I put my trust in thee.
> In God, whose word I praise,
> in God I trust without a fear.
> What can flesh do to me? (vv. 3, 4).

After referring to the threats of his enemies he continued:

> This I know, that God is for me.
> In God, whose word I praise,
> in the Lord, whose word I praise,
> in God I trust without a fear.
> What can man do to me? (vv. 9-11).

In his trials and difficulties he found God to be more than adequate for his needs.

Then there are the familiar words of Psalm 121. Here the psalmist looks to God as the One who can satisfy his every need and longing.

> I lift up my eyes to the hills.
> From whence does my help come?
> My help comes from the Lord,
> who made heaven and earth.

He will not let your foot be moved,
he who keeps you will not slumber.
Behold, he who keeps Israel
will neither slumber nor sleep.

The Lord is your keeper;
the Lord is your shade
on your right hand.
The sun shall not smite you by day,
nor the moon by night.

The Lord will keep you from all evil;
he will keep your life.
The Lord will keep
your going out and your coming in
from this time forth and for evermore.

We can also point to Psalm 91 which speaks
of dwelling in the shelter of the Most High.

Turning to the New Testament we may affirm
that everything which is taught there about the
grace of God presupposes the adequacy of God.
Only he who is totally adequate can be
consistently and always merciful to his
creatures. This certainly was Paul's conviction
as he wrote these words to the church in Rome:
"If God is for us, who is against us? He who did
not spare his own Son but gave him up for us
all, will he not also give us all things with him?"
(Rom. 8:31, 32). The evidence he had already
provided led him to expect a firm "yes" as the
answer.

Earlier in Romans 8 Paul had taught that God
is adequate to meet our every need. By the

gracious activity of the Holy Trinity our present and future needs are met. First of all, the grace of God has the answer to our guilt for sins committed and for the power which sin has over us (Rom. 8:1-9). Through the sacrificial death and resurrection of the incarnate Son, God has made a way by which our sins are forgiven: by "sending his own Son in the likeness of sinful flesh and for sin, he condemned sin in the flesh ..." (Rom. 8:3). And through the presence of the Holy Spirit in the heart we are given the power to live in a way which pleases God.

Second, the grace of God is more than adequate to meet the reality of death (Rom. 8:9-13). For the Christian there is no need to fear either the act of dying or that which lies beyond death: "If the Spirit of him who raised Jesus from the dead dwells in you, he who raised Christ Jesus from the dead will give life to your mortal bodies also through his Spirit which dwells in you" (Rom. 8:11). The Christian has the certain hope of both eternal life and the resurrection of the body at the end of the age (1 Cor. 15).

Third, the grace of God is more than adequate to assist us in our suffering as members of a world which is constantly experiencing suffering (Rom. 8:16-25). We dealt with this topic in our discussion of God as loving. Paul wrote: "I consider that the sufferings of this present time are not worth comparing with the glory that is to be revealed to us" (Rom. 8:18). God has placed his Spirit within our hearts and his presence is a sure guarantee of the fullness of eternal life that will be ours.

Fourth, the grace of God is more than adequate to help us as we seek to pray to God (Rom. 8:26, 27). "We do not know how to pray as we ought, but the Spirit himself intercedes for us with sighs too deep for words" (Rom. 8:26). Paul is not teaching that we are to abandon the normal method of praying for others; rather he is saying that when we sincerely make the effort to pray in love for others, the Holy Spirit will actually assist us and present our prayers to God through Jesus Christ.

Finally, the grace of God is more than adequate to give meaning and purpose to our living (Rom. 8:28-30). What a marvelous assurance is contained in verse 28: "We know that in everything God works for good with those who love him, who are called according to his purpose." Even when we make mistakes God somehow turns the situation around in such a way that we can benefit from it.

Perhaps this theme can be further illustrated by looking at two specific statements of Paul. The first is from 1 Corinthians 10:13: "No temptation has overtaken you that is not common to man. God is faithful, and he will not let you be tempted beyond your strength, but with the temptation will also provide the way of escape, that you may be able to endure it." The Greek word which is translated here "temptation" can also mean "trial." A trial comes from God who wants to purify his children by testing them (e.g., the testing of Abraham concerning the offering of his son). A temptation comes from the devil and its purpose is to seduce people into sin (e.g., the temptations of Jesus were intended to cause him to abandon the will of the Father). Possibly Paul had both trial and temptation in mind here. Since God is faithful toward his people and is all-powerful, he will not allow the devil to overpower the believer. Rather, while allowing the believer to benefit from the experience of temptation (or trial) he will provide a means of escape from it (as in the case of Abraham). So the believer experiences the adequacy of God in such situations.

The second statement is a direct word of the Lord Jesus to Paul: "My grace is sufficient for you, for my power is made perfect in weakness" (2 Cor. 12:9). Paul's response to this was to state that "I will all the more gladly boast of my weaknesses, that the power of Christ may rest upon me. For the sake of Christ, then, I am content with weaknesses, insults, hardships, persecutions, and calamities; for when I am weak, then I am strong." The context here is Paul's description of his repeated request to God that his "thorn in the flesh" which was caused by satanic assaults and which was obviously a great trial to him, should be removed. Whatever the "thorn in the flesh" was exactly, it was God's will that it remain with Paul. Yet in the pain which the "thorn" caused, Paul was assured of the adequacy of God to help him live with, and even rejoice in, his problem. The way in which he told the church of Corinth of his own experience was meant to assure the members that they too could and should know the sufficiency of the grace of God in their experience of life. And, of course, the same is true of us today whatever our trials are.

GOD IS THE SUFFICIENT EXPLANATION FOR ALL THAT IS

Those who trust in God know that he is the perfectly adequate explanation for the universe and everything in it. In claiming this we do not in any way prohibit the work of the various types of scientists as they investigate the composition of our universe and the living creatures who inhabit it. We claim that the God who is revealed in the Bible, Yahweh, the holy, loving, and righteous Lord, is in himself and by himself the perfect explanation for our existence. We leave scientists to describe the world in which we live but we claim with Paul that in God "we live and move and have our being" (Acts 17:28). Scientists alter their theories as they learn more about the universe, but God does not change and that is the reason why all our human questioning about the origin and meaning of life leads us ultimately back to God.

We do not, of course, make God the author of sin. The explanation for sin is to be sought in the fact that God made human beings free, free to obey and free to disobey. Since they chose to disobey (Gen. 2—3), sin came into the world.

Some people will accuse us of participating in wish-fulfillment in our claim that God is the adequate explanation of all reality. They will say that our conviction is not different in kind to that of the Afrikaaner in South Africa who steadfastly believes in the maintenance of apartheid because he wants to preserve the superiority of the Whites over the Bantu. To such an accusation we answer that merely because belief in God satisfies our minds and hearts, it is not thereby rendered false belief. We need to be aware that popular, "intellectual" thinking in our Western society today is dominated by skepticism and cynicism. So the tendency around us is toward the denial rather than the affirmation of God.

Then also our faith in God is under pressure today from what may be called "psychological intimidation." In other words, our motives for belief in God and his adequacy to meet all our deepest needs are challenged on supposed psychological grounds. It is suggested that we have weaknesses of one kind or another in our personalities and characters and we need the idea of a gracious God to make us into adequate people who can face the stress of life. Our motives, it is claimed, are not genuine. This kind of talk is like hitting an opponent below the belt in boxing. A simple reply is to question the psychological motivation of our accusers for their agnosticism or their atheism.

We believe that when we found God (or, more correctly, when God found us), we also found truth. God is adequate in the sense that he is the living God who, as we relate to him, meets our every need "according to his riches in glory in Christ Jesus" (Phil. 4:19). God is adequate, also, in that he is Truth. His reality satisfies the intellectual questionings as well as the spiritual desires and needs of human beings. The longings of our hearts and the probing of our minds will only be and can only be satisfied by the Lord.

TEN
God Is Magnetic

We sometimes sing, "Draw me nearer, nearer, nearer blessed Lord to thy precious bleeding side" and "Nearer my God to thee, nearer to thee." In making this prayer we are not thinking of nearness in terms of distance, but nearness in terms of relationship. We are desiring to be made more aware of the presence of God the Holy Spirit around, through, and in us. This is using language in the same way as when a father states that his son has grown nearer to him as they have both grown older.

To pray to be more conscious of God's presence is to believe that God is attractive. "O taste and see that the Lord is good," sang the psalmist. Frederick Faber, the hymnwriter, wrote:

Only to sit and think of God,
O what a joy it is!
To think the thought, to breathe the Name,
Earth has no higher bliss.

Father of Jesus, love's reward!
What rapture will it be,
Prostrate before thy throne to lie,
And gaze and gaze on thee.

Bernard of Clairvaux also found God attractive:

We taste thee, O thou living Bread,
And long to feast upon thee still:
We drink of thee, the fountainhead,
And thirst our souls from thee to fill.

In this final chapter our purpose is to show that
to know God and to have fellowship with him is
more important than anything else.

RELIGION AND THEOLOGY ARE ATTRACTIVE

Many Christians enjoy attending religious
conventions, conferences, campaigns, and
special meetings. They delight to sing the songs
of Zion, to hear the eloquent Bible teacher, and
to have fellowship with people of similar beliefs.
In moderation such attendance can be helpful.
But "meetings" must never be allowed to
become the substitute for cultivating the
presence of God and knowing him.

It is possible for holy things (as well as material
things) to become a substitute for the holy God
in our lives and experience. Jesus taught that the
truly happy person is the one who is "poor in
spirit" and "pure in heart" (Matt. 5:1-11). Such
a person has learned that the way to God is not
through an abundance of Christian activities or

journeys, but through the development of spiritual receptivity, which involves denial of the human ego. "If any man would come after me," said Jesus, "let him deny himself and take up his cross and follow me. For whoever would save his life will lose it; and whoever loses his life for my sake and the gospel's will save it" (Mark 8:34, 35).

Holy things and activities become a substitute for the holy God because the life of God has not been nurtured and nourished in our souls. Egoistic sins are still in prominence—self-righteousness, self-confidence, self-sufficiency, self-admiration, and self-interest. Sadly, the manifestation of these are tolerated in Christian leaders who are admired and who speak from many a platform. Exhibitionism and self-promotion are very common in certain Christian circles. Promoting self under the guise of promoting Christ is often so common as to excite little comment. If this is the case among leaders, then how difficult it is to blame those who are led. To elevate or promote self is to make a veil which hides the face of God from us and prevents the realization of the prayer, "Draw me nearer, blessed Lord . . ."

For some Christians (a smaller number than those attracted by the endless round of religious meetings), theology is attractive. We all know that it is possible to study Christian theology without ever being a Christian; we sometimes accuse some of our professional theologians who work in universities and colleges of being in this category. Most of us have friends who gain great pleasure in discussing the date and nature of the Millennium and second coming of Christ, or such topics as predestination and free-will. It is possible for us to enjoy debating and studying theology as we enjoy studying any other subject. And, strangely, the more difficult areas of doctrine seem to have a peculiar fascination for some minds. But we must not deceive ourselves. To know theological doctrines or even to know biblical verses is not the same as to know God in personal fellowship. Knowing about God, though necessary, is not equivalent to knowing God.

The attendance at meetings and the study of theology are both meant to be means to an end, not an end in themselves. Christian fellowship and worship are to lead each of us nearer to God. Christian theology is to inform the mind about God so that we may love and serve him as he wishes. We must beware of the attractiveness of meetings and doctrines as things in themselves and only make use of them in our pursuit of God himself.

DRAWING NEARER TO GOD

God is a Person. In a way in which we cannot fully understand he thinks, wills, desires, loves, and communicates. He enters into relationships with us and we experience him in our minds, wills, and emotions. To know God in terms of personal fellowship is to have eternal life, for God is eternal (John 17:3).

It is God who begins this personal relationship.

God the Father calls us through God the Son in the power of God the Holy Spirit. He puts within us a new nature and with it come new thoughts, new intentions, and new desires which are all God-centered. Yet God does not eradicate the old self in us It remains and we are called by God's assistance to live, not by the old standards associated with the old self, but by the standards of the Holy Spirit (Gal. 5:16-26). This means to live for God according to the demands he places upon us and which Jesus outlined in the Sermon on the Mount.

Drawing nearer to God is not achieved overnight. Our spiritual awareness has to be cultivated and developed. Receptivity to God is deepened gradually. God becomes more and more attractive as our receptivity to him increases. Failure to recognize this is the cause of much misunderstanding of the nature of the Christian life in modern, activist Christianity. We live in a technological society where many things are instamatic or automatic. We are impatient of slower and more tedious ways of achieving what we want. And we make a big mistake when we apply this type of thinking to our relationship with God. We do not draw near to God merely by the five-minute daily devotion or the enthusiasm of a religious meeting.

There is no shortcut to a growing awareness of the presence of God. We must prayerfully make use of the normal means of grace (local church worship and fellowship); we must read our Bibles slowly and thoroughly; we must be quiet and seek to cultivate an awareness of the

One who says, "Be still, and know that I am God" (Psa. 46:10); we must discipline ourselves not to neglect prayer, meditation, and self-examination. Above all, we must submit ourselves to God so that he can gradually make us to be "poor in spirit," "meek," and "pure in heart"—that Christ may be formed in us. God delights to make himself known to the humble (Luke 10:21, 22). And we need always to be aware of the subtle temptations that come to us through the culture in which we live.

By God's help (and he longs to help us) we need to be constantly in the position which the psalmist knew when he wrote:

As a hart longs
for flowing streams,
so longs my soul
for thee, O God.
My soul thirsts for God,
for the living God (Psa. 42:1, 2).

Paul expressed a similar theme when he wrote of his desire to know Christ "and the power of his resurrection, and [to] share his sufferings, becoming like him in his death . . ." (Phil. 3:10). The nearer the saints come to God the more attractive he becomes to them, and so they pray to be drawn even nearer.

THE VISION OF GOD

Jesus said, "Blessed are the pure in heart, for they shall see God" (Matt. 5:8). Such people will

172

certainly see God in the life of heaven. Also they see God now, by faith, in this world.

They see God in and through the created world and can sing:

> Heaven above is softer blue,
> Earth beneath is sweeter green,
> Something lives in every hue
> Christless eyes have never seen.

They see him making the clouds his chariot and riding on the wings of the wind (Psa. 104:3); they see him making the grass grow for the cattle and plants for man to cultivate that he may bring forth food from the earth and wine to gladden the heart of man (Psa. 104:14, 15). And they know that he is upholding all things by the word of his power (Heb. 1:3).

At the personal level they see God guiding and directing their lives, in sickness and health, in riches and poverty, and in youth and old age. They know his hand is over them for good. They are confident that he knows the minutest details of their lives, even the number of hairs upon their bodies (Matt. 10:30). They are sure that "in everything God works for good with those who love him, who are called according to his purpose" (Rom. 8:28).

They especially see God through the means of grace which he has appointed. When they join with others to worship him in the beauty of holiness (1 Chron. 16:29), and when they meet around the Lord's Table to eat bread and drink wine (1 Cor. 11) they see God. And they talk to

him "face to face, as a man speaks to his friend"
(Exod. 33:11). They also see God when they
withdraw to the quiet of their private rooms to
pray and search the Scriptures (Matt. 6:6).

Let us pray that daily we shall see God:

Almighty God,
to whom all hearts are open,
all desires known,
and from whom no secrets are hid:
cleanse the thoughts of our hearts
by the inspiration of your Holy Spirit,
that we may perfectly love you,
and worthily magnify your holy name;
through Christ our Lord. Amen.

APPENDIX:
The Church Doctrine of the Holy Trinity

The writers of the New Testament never doubted that the One to whom they prayed as Father was their living God. Also, they came to see that Jesus Christ is God in human flesh and that the Holy Spirit is the personal, present reality of God. In the New Testament there are occasions when Father and Son and Holy Spirit are linked closely together: 1 Peter 1:2; 2 Thessalonians 2:13, 14; Titus 3:4-6; Jude 20, 21. The following passages refer to the joint work of Father, Son, and Holy Spirit: Galatians 1:3, 4; Ephesians 1; 4:4, 5; 1 Corinthians 12:4-6. (Other verses worth looking at are Matt. 12:28; Mark 1:10, 11; Luke 1:35; John 1:33, 34; 20:21, 22; Acts 2:33, 38, 39; Rom. 8:11; 15:16, 30; 2 Cor. 1:21, 22; Gal. 4:6; Eph. 2:18; 1 John 4:13, 14.)

Many Christians in and after the days of the apostles were quite content to accept the reality of God—Father, Son and Holy Spirit—and ask no searching questions about his reality. How he could be Three in One and One in Three did not seem to be a problem to them. They simply took the revelation within the New Testament at its face value.

THE TRUTH ABOUT THE RELATION OF JESUS CHRIST TO GOD THE FATHER

Christians, and especially their leaders, were forced to ask questions concerning God in Trinity for the simple reason that members of the churches began to teach what were obviously errors about the reality of God. One famous pastor named Arius (250-336) who worked in Alexandria in Egypt taught what appeared (to people living in a Greek cultural environment) an attractive doctrine of God. His doctrine has many similarities with that of the present-day Jehovah's Witnesses. Arius believed that God himself is so far above and beyond us that he could not enter into our space and time. He is totally beyond our universe. Jesus Christ was not the Son of God entering into our universe and assuming manhood; rather he was the incarnation of an angel or archangel. If God is beyond our universe and cannot enter it, then Jesus Christ cannot be God, argued Arius. Therefore, he must be a kind of superior creature made by God.

The teaching of Arius, often reduced to the contents of popular religious choruses, proved so popular that it spread like wildfire among the churches. It caused so much trouble that the Emperor Constantine decided that the church leaders should meet to discuss it. This they did at the town of Nicea (which is fifty miles east of modern Istanbul) and their meeting is usually called the first ecumenical council, since bishops from many parts of the Roman world were assembled.

The major question which this council faced was: what is the truth about the relation of Jesus Christ to God the Father? Arius had forced this question into the open and now an answer had to be given. There was no escape from this question. The bishops and theologians in the council would have loved to have given their answer in biblical verses and terms. However, they had to face the important fact that Arius and his supporters (like modern Jehovah's Witnesses) always quoted verses from the Bible. (Arius quoted especially Prov. 8:22; Acts 2:36; Rom. 8:29; Heb. 3:2, and John 14:28. If you look these up you will see why Arius could say that Jesus Christ is inferior to the Father and is a creature. Of course, his opponents answered that these verses had to be understood in the context of the total message of the Bible and not as isolated statements.)

Therefore, very reluctantly, the members of the council decided that they would have to use some nonbiblical words and phrases in order to convey the truth as they saw it. For them the truth was this: that which is true of the Father is also true of the Son, except that the Son is not the Father and the Father is not the Son. In other words, the Son is as much God as is the Father, and the Father is as much God as is the Son. So they produced a creed. (This creed was rewritten at the next ecumenical council at Constantinople in 381, but it is usually called the Nicene Creed, and is in wide use in Christian churches today.) Let us read the central paragraph which explains that relation of the Father and the Son.

> We believe in one Lord Jesus Christ, the Son of God, *begotten* from the Father, only-begotten, that is, from the *substance* of the Father, God from God, Light from Light, true God from true God, begotten not made, *of one substance* with the Father, through Whom all things came into being, things in heaven and things on earth, Who because of us men and because of our salvation came down from heaven and became incarnate, becoming man, suffered and rose again on the third day, ascended to the heavens, and will come to judge the living and the dead.

We need to look closely at two words: "begotten" and "substance." The Greek word which is here translated as "substance" is *ousia* and the phrase "of one substance with" translated the word *homoousios* (which is an extension of *ousia*). Now if you place near to each other three branches from one tree you can say that "they share the same substance (*ousia*) which is wood." You can also say that one branch is of one substance with another of the branches. *Ousia* is that which several things

178

have in common. By saying that the Father and the Son have the same *ousia,* the bishops at the council were stating that whatever deity the Father has is also shared by the Son. To help them state this important fact they had made use of a term from Greek philosophy. They had used a nonbiblical expression in the service of what they regarded as the truth of God.

Now let us look at the word "begotten." When we think of how a child comes into this world we think of him being begotten by his father and born from his mother. The human father through sexual intercourse with the mother begets the son, who because of this physical relationship bears some characteristics of the father. The father passes on his nature to the son through the mother. When the bishops used this word in their Creed, they did so because they found it used by John in his Gospel (1:13, 14). Certainly they were not using the word in its normal, earthly sense, but rather only to emphasize the relation between Father and Son in the Godhead. They wanted to emphasize that the eternal being of the Father is eternally shared by the Son. Christians are sons of God by adoption; the Son is the only-begotten that is unique Son, for eternally he shares the being of the Father. The Father is eternally sharing with the Son or passing on to the Son his deity.

So the council affirmed, in the language which for them made the best sense, that Jesus Christ was truly the Son of God in human flesh; not an archangel made into a man, but the Son of God made man. In the last analysis such a truth is beyond our understanding, but it is a basic theme in the New Testament.

QUESTIONS ARISE ABOUT THE HOLY SPIRIT

Having affirmed that the Father and the Son share the same deity, the question "What about the Holy Spirit?" inevitably arose. Thus the church leaders had to answer this question. Their task was made the more urgent because a certain Macedonius (c. 362), a bishop in Constantinople, taught that the Holy Spirit was inferior to the Father and the Son and was in fact a creature made by God.

So at the Council of Constantinople in 381 the assembled bishops worked out the following statement which became a part of the Creed of Nicea (Nicene Creed):

We believe in the Holy Spirit, the Lord and life-giver, Who proceeds from the Father, Who with the Father and the Son is together worshiped and glorified, Who spoke through the prophets ...

Here the Holy Spirit is given the title of Lord (*Kyrios*), is said to be the giver of eternal life (which only God can give) and to proceed from the Father even as the Son proceeds from the Father. Further he is to be worshiped and to be glorified as God.

Regrettably, after the Council of Constantinople, while the churches of the Eastern and

Western halves of the Roman Empire agreed in affirming the deity of the Holy Spirit and giving to him proper worship, they disagreed theologically on the precise way his relation to the Father and Son should be stated. So each side amended the Creed. In the East it was held that the Holy Spirit proceeds from the Father *through* the Son (and this is still the belief of the Greek and Russian Orthodox Churches) while in the West it was held that the Holy Spirit proceeds from the Father *and* the Son (and this is still the belief of the Roman Catholic and virtually all Protestant churches).

For ordinary people this verbal difference is without importance. It belongs to highly developed theological thinking and expresses different ways of seeing the truth of God.

THE CLASSIC WESTERN DOCTRINE OF THE HOLY TRINITY

The doctrine of the Trinity as expressed in the Confessions of Faith of the Protestant Churches (Anglican, Lutheran, Presbyterian, etc.) as well as the Roman Catholic owes its exposition primarily to the great theologian, Augustine of Hippo (354—430). Starting from the teaching of the Nicene Creed of 381, he expounded this doctrine in careful detail in a Latin book entitled, *De Trinitate*, written in 416. The contents cannot be easily summarized here. However, there exists (in part of a creed called the Athanasian Creed, which dates from a few years after Augustine) a careful summary of

Augustine's main points. Here is the opening section:

> The Catholic Faith is this: That we worship one God in Trinity and Trinity in Unity; neither confounding the *Persons*; nor dividing the *Substance*. For there is one Person of the Father, another of the Son and another of the Holy Ghost. But the Godhead of the Father, of the Son and of the Holy Spirit is all one: the glory equal, the majesty co-eternal.

There are two technical words which call for comment, one is "substance" and the other is "Persons." The word substance occurs in the Nicene Creed and already we have looked at its meaning. In that creed the Father and the Son are said to share the same "substance;" here the statement is extended for all three; Father, Son, and Spirit share the same "substance." Whatever deity the Father has is also possessed by both Son and Spirit.

The other word is more difficult to explain. In our modern use of language the word person usually means an individual who has a specific personality and a certain appearance. Person, personality, and character seem to be closely associated. When this word was used in the creed, the Latin word *persona* did not carry these modern meanings. Rather it meant something like "separate identity" and was used to emphasize that while there is one God, he has three true and separate identities. If we read this creed and think of "person" in a modern sense then we will misunderstand what is being said. Person as used in the creed means an individual mode of being. Thus we say that God is Three in One, and One in Three. This is a true mystery which we shall never fully be able to explain. We believe it because the biblical evidence leads us to this conclusion.

(The use of the word "person" of God is further complicated because rightly we claim that "God is personal." By this claim we mean that God is ready and able to enter into relationships with people; because he can enter into relationships with people he must be (in a very exalted way) personal. Here the word person is not being used in the technical sense of the creed; rather it is being used in what we may call a common-sense way.)

THE DOCTRINE OF THE TRINITY TODAY

By this time the reader is probably feeling that this doctrine is rather difficult to understand. So questions arise: Do we really need to know the Church doctrine of the Trinity today? Is it sufficient to know what the Bible teaches about "the grace of the Lord Jesus, the love of God the Father, and the fellowship of the Holy Spirit"? The answer to these questions will vary according to the place a Christian holds in his congregation and/or denomination.

Take the ordinary member of a church who finds study difficult but who is an able artisan. He reads his Bible daily with the help of appropriate aids (e.g., notes) and prays that God will guide him. Such a man is under no kind of obligation to study the Church doctrine of the Trinity. Rather he is to believe what he reads in the Bible about Father, Son, and Holy Spirit. And, if he is a faithful Christian in his experience of God, he will *know* him as God, the Father, who loves him; God, the Son, the Savior, who redeems him; and God, the Holy Spirit, who lives within him. It surely is a fact that thousands of Christians have lived faithful lives who have never understood, intellectually, what the doctrine of the Trinity really means. Yet, since in faith they are joined to this God who is One in Three, they have known him in that full sense of having fellowship with him.

But the case is different with the man or woman who is a leader in a church. Pastors and teachers and other people in positions of leadership should have a knowledge both of the biblical and the Church doctrine of the Trinity. Here are several reasons for stating this:

1. The Church doctrine of the Trinity represents the result of four centuries of intense study of Scripture by very able minds. Great minds since then have felt obliged to accept the doctrine as required by Scripture.

2. Over the centuries the Church has found by experience that the only way fully to preserve the doctrines that Jesus Christ is God incarnate, and that the Spirit within the Church is God, is to confess the doctrine that God is One in Three.

3. The doctrine of the Trinity proves very helpful as a key to unlocking the treasures of the Bible as we read it. To know that God's internal

life is trinitarian is to gain insight into his total revelation to mankind. For example, the revelation of the divine name to Moses as "I AM THAT I AM" means much more when we know that God is One in Three and Three in One.

4. When we know this doctrine we are able quickly to recognize the major heresies or false teachings which regularly plague the Church. Therefore in knowing this doctrine the Christian pastor, teacher, or leader is better able to exercise the gifts God has given him/her for the good of the flock of Christ.

SELECT
BIBLIOGRAPHY

1. Two excellent popular books are R. T. France, *The Living God* (London: Inter-Varsity Press, 1970); and J. I. Packer, *Knowing God* (Downers Grove, IL: InterVarsity Press, 1975).

2. For the biblical basis for the doctrine of the Trinity, the best introduction is Arthur W. Wainwright, *The Trinity in the New Testament* (Naperville, IL: Allenson, 1962).

3. The best introduction to the development of the doctrine of God in the first five centuries is J. N. Kelly, *Early Christian Doctrine* (New York: Harper & Row Pubs., Inc., 4th ed., 1976). It gives the background to the Nicene and Athanasian Creeds.

4. A classic book is Augustine's *On the Trinity*, which is best read in the Library of Christian Classics, Volume 8, edited by John Burnaby in 1955. Also worthy of study is Book 1 of John Calvin's *Institutes of the Christian Religion* (Grand Rapids, MI: Wm. B. Eerdmans Pub. Co., 1953).

5. An often-reprinted Puritan presentation is Stephen Charnock's *The Existence and Attributes of God*, while Harman Bavinck's *The Doctrine of God* (Grand Rapids, MI: Baker Book House, 1977) is a solid study written over half a century ago.

6. For those with philosophical interests and who wish to examine various views as to the nature of God (pantheism, panentheism, etc.), H. P. Owen's *Concepts of Deity* (London: Macmillan, 1971) is excellent. So also, in introducing the reader to the nature of faith in God is George I. Mavrodes, *Belief in God* (Westminster, MD: Random House, Inc., 1970).

7. There is a growing literature on the relationship of Christianity to other religions. Here two books may be recommended as starters: Stephen Neill, *Salvation Tomorrow* (Nashville: Abingdon Press, 1976) and E. Sharpe, *Faith Meets Faith* (London: S.C.M., 1977).

8. For an introduction to the problem of suffering, see Brian Hebbletwaite, *Evil, Suffering and Religion* (New York: Hawthorn Books, Inc., 1976).

9. On the relation of evolution and creation see Ian G. Barbour, *Issues in Science and Religion* (New York: Harper & Row Pubs., Inc., 1971), especially chapters 4 and 12; and D. S. Spanner, *Creation and Evolution* (London: Falcon Books, 1965).

10. For the pursuit of God as attractive to mind and heart, a good starting point is Augustine's famous book, *Confessions*, which is available in a variety of editions.

11. For the presentation of the doctrine of God in Scripture see George A. F. Knight, *A Christian Theology of the Old Testament* (London: SCM Press Ltd., 1964); and George E. Ladd, *A Theology of the New Testament* (Grand Rapids, MI: Wm. B. Eerdmans Pub. Co., 1974).

12. On the theme that God speaks through Scripture by the Holy Spirit see Leon Morris, *I Believe in Revelation* (Grand Rapids, MI: Wm. B. Eerdmans Pub. Co., 1976); and R. M. Horn, *The Book That Speaks for Itself* (London: Inter-Varsity Press, 1974).